LIVING COMMUNITY, LIVING SCHOOL

D1638295

LIVING COMMUNITY, LIVING SCHOOL

Essays on Education in British inner cities

Chris Searle

the Tufnell Press

the Tufnell Press,
47 Dalmeny Road,
London, N7 0DY

First published 1997

British Library Cataloguing-in-Publication Data
A catalogue record for this book is
available from the British Library

ISBN 1 872767 27 3

Printed in England by Da Costa Print, London

Contents

Acknowledgements

In such a book as this, many people contribute. My particular thanks go to the students, governors and communities of Earl Marshal School in Sheffield, for their words and creative sparks are the book's foundation.

My gratitude too, goes to my friends at the Institute if Race Relations, London, and to the Editor and Deputy Editor of its international Journal, *Race and Class*. Several of the essays that follow first saw publication there, and the editorial criticisms of A. Siranandan and Hazel Waters, always improved my work.

I would also like to thank many other friends and colleagues who helped and stood up for me over difficult years. My thanks go particularly to Buzz Johnson, Ahmed Gurnah, Lesley Holly, Bill Moore, Abdul Shaif, Mike Atkins, Derek Rose, Muna Eidaroos, Michael Apple, Mick Poore, Sue Bower and Mary Burdon. And to Pearl and the boys, for everything they give.

A version of *'Only a pencil': The centrality of Literacy* appeared in Colin Lankshear and Peter McLaren (Eds.): *Critical Literacy*, Suny Press, New York, 1993.

Living Community, Living School is dedicated to the memory of young school student, poet and cricketer, Izat Khan, 1976-1992. May his metaphors and his off drives surprise heaven. It is also dedicated to Eddie Coupe, colleague, friend and deputy headteacher of Earl Marshal School who died in post in November 1995.

PREFACE

There was a time when teaching was a vocation, not an occupation, and education not the imparting of information merely, but the eliciting of every conceivable possibility of the human mind and soul. Children were the measure of our possibilities, their minds such forests of imagination that even political backwoodsmen took care to spare the trees.

No more. The Social Darwinists are among us. At every stage of schooling, there is selection and segregation and sanitisation—through the opting out of schools, tests and exclusions, and the national curriculum. The opting out system, by allowing schools to opt out of local authority control, allows them to opt out of their obligation to cater to all the children in their catchment area, and select, instead, those whom the schools feel will bring them the results that ensure continued government funding. And since such selection often involves interviews with parents, the children of the less well-educated parents have less chance of getting in than those of the better educated—thereby reproducing the cycle of deprivation. Hence, by simply shifting the emphasis of schooling from the needs of the child (for education) to the needs of the school (for results, productivity, value for money), opting out helps to bring back Victorian class differences and structure them into the schools system itself.

And the tests reinforce such structured inequality further—at two levels. Firstly, they select out the supposedly bright children from the not-so-bright at 7 and 11 and 14 and 16, formalising, and regimenting thereby, the free growth of the child. Secondly, they select out the good (i.e. achieving) schools from the bad (i.e. non-achieving) schools and, by listing them in a league table of success, ensure that the better schools attract the more successful children. Tests, in effect, measure the progress of the school by measuring the progress of the child, and so privilege the school with privileged children—thereby sealing off the economic and social mobility that education is meant to offer the less privileged.

While tests segregate on the basis of achievement, exclusions segregate on the basis of behaviour, which, in a racist society, becomes structured in cultural or racial terms—thereby compounding class disability with racial disadvantage in a process of social cleansing.

Finally, there is the national curriculum, which, both in its choice of core subjects—'there's a common culture, so we have a core curriculum' (Jack Straw)—and in their teaching—'Britain has a great and inspiring heritage; our children need to be fed on it'

(S. Pearce)—sanitizes the whole learning process and deprives children of the critical spirit which enables them to be the future custodians of our democracy.

Against this tide of dis-education stand a handful of far-sighted educationalists, among whom has to be counted the ex-Head of Earl Marshal School in Sheffield. During the five years that he was there, Chris Searle brought out his students' passion for learning, sharpened the edge of their curiosity, enlarged their horizons and vision, gave them authority over their own experiences enriched by the experiences of other cultures and taught them, with Keats, to honour 'the holiness the heart's affection and the truth of the imagination'. It is there in the books of verse and prose and prose poems that the students of Earl Marshal School have produced—in *Valley of Words*, *School of the World* , *Lives of Love and Hope* and *Heart of Sheffield* and in their researches on Sheffield's racism.

But then Chris Searle believes in children, and he believes in education—and children believe in him, for he is that curious mix of guru, guerilla and your favourite fast bowler.

A . Sivanandan
Director, Institute of Race Relations, London
Editor, *Race and Class*

INTRODUCTION

This book is published at a time when much emphasis is being placed on the restoration of 'morality' in the British school system. This ought to be a timely debate, for schools throughout the country, particularly those in our inner cities, are staggering under the moral barbarism of the market system of education, to the same degree that the most vulnerable people living and surviving in the same inner cities— have gradually felt the economic and social conditions of their lives worsen around them.

Yet the 'moral crusade' embraced by the powerful and prestigious—from party leaders, to royalty, to church hierarchies and media barons—has ignored the central issue of the destructive impact of market forces upon people's lives. 'Morality' has been re-interpreted, then changed and debased to 'moralism', when meanings of right and wrong have been forced into rhetoric and camouflage, and the central factor of market chaos and arbitrariness being unleashed into people's lives has been covered over. When the proponents of an education system built around rampant individualism and threat of failure, selection, exclusion and a uniform narrowness of knowledge rail against 'immorality' and 'evil', demonising the young for the cruelty and violence that they, the rulers, institutionalised and made systemic, then it is a sign that their obsession with 'morality' and 'moral crusades' is little more than a fig leaf to hide the immorality which they themselves have created and control.

Morality demeaned

For what is 'morality' in education, how is it manifested by a school in the British inner city? The reality is not promising. Certainly, by the standards and aims accepted by the rest of the world through the 1989 United Nations Convention on the Rights of the Child, we are experiencing a serious slippage. Even the moral right to a free and universal state education is at serious risk, as thousands of British school students are 'permanently excluded' from school, the majority of whom never enter another school. The alliance of school with the right to fundamental sustenance and health provision is also breached with the end of free school milk (achieved by Margaret Thatcher when she was Secretary of State for Education) and the real threat to withdraw free school meals from the most vulnerable and frequently the most hungry—the daughters and sons of refugees and asylum seekers. How can these measures square with 'morality', and how can the right of an education for peace sit with the present Secretary of State for Education's support for the restoring of corporal punishment in schools and a Prime Ministerial promotion of cadet forces and gun training in every school, in the aftermath of the school killings by a crazed gunman in Dunblane? How does this connect with the 'moral crusade' if not to demean and subvert it from its conception? And how can a pursuit of education for equal opportunity—a basic moral pursuit—be reconciled with greater budgetary allocations for grant maintained schools and the creation of a hierarchy of schools through the establishment of city technology colleges and the promise of 'a grammar school in every town'? Or how can a market system, dependent upon the success of the few at the cost of the failure of the many, the 'league table' mentality and the scramble of each school for more pupil heads against its neighbour be deemed 'a moral system' by any belief system with a coherent code of right and wrong? And with the stringency of the narrow 'orders' of National Curriculum and the state control of school knowledge, how can we forward the participation rights of children, their freedom to express their own view and body of knowledge with their basic right to make their words active in matters affecting their own lives, for these too are threatened to be 'ordered out'.

In the British context, the tragic truth is that the 'opposition' Labour Party—now under a 'New Labour' leadership—would have been expected to be the guardian of these rights and resources, and restore and consolidate them upon their re-entry into government. In fact they guarantee a continuation of the Conservative restoration in education as in other areas of social policy such as the Police Bill (with its new denials of civil liberties) and trades union 'reform', promising to retain the market system of schooling and its edifice of Kenneth Baker's 1988 Education Act, the National Curriculum, league tables, testing at seven, eleven, fourteen and sixteen, the undemocratic and powerful education quangos, OFSTED and the sharp divisions and 'diversity' within the school system—with the children of the New Labour leader and a powerful shadow cabinet colleague attending exclusive grant maintained schools long distances from their homes. Such is an indication of the probable 'morality' to come. For instead of attacking poverty and standing up for the most beleaguered and oppressed, they too propose to castigate the undeserving poor—the beggars, the never-employed, the single mothers, the 'squeegee merchants', the housing estate youth they propose to curfew, the excluded and alienated from school, the refugees and the homeless—and cover the gulf of class reality with pious statements of virtue and moralism. The movement for socialism becomes a middle class and populist moral crusade: the struggle for justice through education is replaced by the pursuit of authoritarian 'decency' and the further exclusion of the rejected, rebellious and 'disruptive'. The poor and already marginalised and demotivated are threatened to be pushed completely off the page.

A new masquerade

On the same page that the *Times*[1] reported on the presentation of a draft document of 'a moral code for schools' from a quango called the 'National Forum for Values in

Education and the Community', it also reported on a parliamentary bill opening the way to Conservative Prime Minister John Major's personal and political dream of much greater school selection and a 'grammar school in every town', restoring the system of minority educational success and majority educational failure that existed so nakedly before the development of comprehensive schools. The 'National Forum' is led by Dr. Nick Tate of the School Curriculum and Assessment Authority, an apologist for a narrow and exclusivist concept of 'national identity' to be imposed upon British children through school life and a strict adherence to the National Curriculum. With such constraints on the burgeoning internationalism of British inner city life and schools, Tate claimed to give the lie to the 'absurd accusation that schools are moral-free zones'.

These events took place while the leader of Britain's second largest teachers' union, Nigel de Gruchy of the National Association of Schoolmasters and Union of Women Teachers (NASUWT), was recommending strike action unless 60 students (10 per cent of the school population) of the Ridings School in Calderdale, Yorkshire, were excluded forthwith, and members of his union were beginning an indefinite strike for the removal of a ten-year-old boy from Manton Junior School in Worksop, Nottinghamshire. The boy's particular crime was that his parents had exercised their democratic rights and won an appeal against their son's permanent exclusion from the school for disruptive behaviour. These actions were taken, claimed the NASUWT, with the objective of restoring moral order to the schools and stemming the tide of 'disruption' and 'violence' within them, by targeting individual students and their families—predominantly working class families who had constantly been the objects of two decades of conservative rule. The records of targeted individual students, their confidential files and documents were suddenly exposed to the national press and for the world to see. The NASUWT had another agenda too: their leadership's single-minded ambition to overtake the membership of their rival union, the National Union of Teachers. As de Gruchy revealed on an article in the *Independent in Sunday*,[2] he was not a trade unionist for the benefit of young people at school. Other forces propelled him: 'Pupils don't pay subscriptions, members do.'

A wider context to this masquerade of 'morality' was the announcement of a 'moral crusade' in schools and its publication firstly in the *Times*[3] of Rupert Murdoch , and subsequently in most of the other establishment papers, by Frances Lawrence, whose late husband, headteacher Phillip Lawrence, had been killed on December 1995 by a local youth, as he bravely went to the assistance of a pupil under attack at his school gates. Mrs. Lawrence made some important points about banning combat knives and instituting a sharper focus within the school curriculum on the meaning of good citizenship, and she found nodding support from the leaders of the three major political parties. The 'crusade' had a strong opportunistic appeal to de Gruchy and the NASUWT leadership, especially as it had been launched in Phillip Lawrence's name and he had been a very 'high excluding' headteacher, making 60 permanent exclusions during the two years that he was in post (which corresponded exactly to the number de Gruchy was calling to be excluded at the Ridings School).[4] Thus the 'moral crusade' was being built upon the uneasy foundations of high rates of permanent exclusion from school: a strategy which, while behaviourally cleansing schools of their 'disruptive' elements and those demotivated and challenging students who take more effort and creative pedagogy to teach, offered the excluded student as food for criminalisation, further disaffection, gang-conflict and an easy prey to drug dealing.

Meanwhile, the establishment press was having many a field day with its heterogeneous stories of feigned moral outrage. Whereas the *Sunday Mirror*[5] concentrated its 'news focus' on violence in schools with a headline (like many others across the tabloid press) that demonised the young, 'Evil behind the innocence: grim truth of the violent reign of terror in our classrooms', its daily sister paper had juxtaposed an article on Mrs. Lawrence's crusade (illustrated by a dignified, colour family photograph of her children and late husband) with a scurrilous and racist article by columnist Tony Parsons on the family of the youth convicted of Phillip Lawrence's murder. The Filipino mother of Learco Chindamo is called a 'stupid cow' whose only interest, we are told is that 'she wanted a deep and meaningful relationship with our welfare state'. She is emblematised as a foreign black licentious mother—the antithesis of Mrs. Lawrence—the unwanted beneficiary of a gulled and milked system which is 'handing out accommodation to any immigrant who wanted it'. Such is the compassion attached to the 'crusade' and the cruel exploitation of Mrs. Lawrence's sincerity and grief.

As for the wide but predictable coverage of the Ridings School, its problems were blamed upon its ranks of 'unteachable' students—not only by the NASUWT but by most elements of the national press. It was left to the minority *Morning Star*[7] to publish an article by the local parliamentarian, Ann Mahon M.P., who explained how Calderdale Education Authority, had presided over a schools *status quo* that was cruelly divided and ineffectual. Two of the LEA's largest secondary schools had been taking extra government funding by 'opting out' to become grant maintained in the eighties, leaving the others, like the Ridings, underinvested, underfunded and stigmatised as inferior. When the Calderdale Council had bid to the government for extra finance for essential improvements to the Ridings through the Single Regeneration Budget, they had been rejected—in short an excellent incident and text to study by the morality-builders of the National Forum for Values in Education, but one which is quite probably beyond their remit.

So whenever there are twisted and market-created situations, you can always blame them upon the 'immorality' and 'evil' of black and working class young people: the system's prime targets and casualties become its demons. And as demons they must exert no control, have no scope for their own 'meaning-making' and democratic choice and participation must be denied them. As Melanie Phillips, a recruit to the crusade, declares in her handbook of rhetorical moralism, *All must have prizes*, 'Democracy is for adults. Choice is adult behaviour', not the property of the young.[8]

The community alternative

The pages that follow seek to show that there is another way, and that it can be taken. The inner city school that is at the heart of the narratives and commentary that follow was certainly beset with the usual problems and privations facing such schools, but tried other strategies to marketeering, exclusion and philosophies of blame and 'evil'. As a school it sought to create a moral groundwork based upon internal and external solidarity that would be worthy of the creative genius and generosity of its students and constituent communities. For its founding and organic connection was with its community—to involve, reflect, affirm and develop it in whatever ways it could, particularly in its *actional* dimension. The school's narrative was the community, and that narrative has morality if it lives for and tells of the people to whom its work is dedicated. That means primarily that the school gives *authority* to its community, it offers reason, involvement, dignity, solidarity and hope. It expresses the values of empathy between its students and their parents and an engendering confidence for the young to emulate the struggles and achievements of those who have come before and cared for them. It is internationalist in its approach to curriculum, cultural and ethical issues, and issues of faith, because its own community is internationalist: its nation is the imagination, the knowledge base that it proposes is multilingual and multidimensional, with a pride in its working class history and its meanings from the many worlds of experience that make up one world. Giving authority to that breadth and depth of experience means going beyond, voyaging out from the narrow, tramlined and blinkered confines of an imposed body of state-licensed knowledge and 'orders' known as the National Curriculum. For this school creates curriculum through the complex interaction and narratives of its own constituents: that is its morality, its code of what is right. And that involves moving through curriculum and propositions of knowledge, towards action: to work at being yourself and being better at being yourself, but seeing and knowing yourself also as part of the world, for your school as a school of the world. This is why, over a five-year span, the young people at this school, often helped and supported by their teachers but mainly through their own commitment and excellence at fund-raising strategies, raised literally thousands of pounds for a free hospital for cancer patients in Pakistan, for the victims of floods in Pakistan and Bangladesh, of cholera in Guyana, war, rape and displacement in Bosnia, illiteracy in Ethiopia, civil destruction in northern Somalia, repression and denial of nationhood in Kashmir and Kurdistan, and the negation of civil rights and asylum in Britain. This was active morality, economic morality—we call it solidarity with other human beings, for that is what it was—taking knowledge into one's brain and seeing it emerge through head and heart as social love and empathy. It began as literacy and poetry: it ended as living and giving.

It is also why the word 'exclusion' became such a hinge word at the school, and such a bitter cause of contention between its teachers. The school's governors and headteacher, plus some loyal and dedicated colleagues, worked to gradually make the word a disappearing concept, to be replaced by that of the *inclusive school*. While the national increase in permanent exclusions was reflected in Sheffield, and a virtual small army of school-age youths were to be seen every day in city centre and local shopping mall venues, calling out from their classrooms even greater numbers of truants, this secondary school, by all statistics and indices serving the most economically disadvantaged neighbourhoods of the city, stayed fast to its principle of 'holding on' to demotivated , angry and sometimes disruptive students, by employing creative strategies that were alternatives to exclusion, (and by doing so saving the LEA thousands of pounds in high-cost 'special education' provision). One of these approaches was to work closely with school governors and the community organisations they represented— the Sheffield and District African-Caribbean Association, the Yemeni Community Association, the Somali Community Association, the Pakistan Muslim Centre—sending students who were 'on the brink' to community centres for work experience, counselling and working within an adult environment in their own community ethos for a fast maturing experience. This method was frequently effective and persuaded some volatile students to behave differently on their return to the school, while drawing the school even closer to its communities.

Keeping consistent with an inclusive approach, the school also welcomed many students expelled from other schools in the city who were finding immense difficulties in being accepted in an alternative school—sometimes for their involvement, usually marginally, with drugs. A part of a high-profile drugs education project was to publicly campaign against a growing drugs menace within the neighbourhood of the school. This was a contrary approach to some Sheffield schools which sought to hide their drugs problems and wish them away by excluding their students, so as not to become tarred in the pupil marketplace. In classes, assemblies and preventative education across the school, a process of critical literacy and understanding began not only to expose the dangers of a drug connection, but to involve all students in its insights. Thus Sarah, horrified at the dangers of infected syringes dropped by local drug users near the school, wrote her striking poem which was read in assemblies and in its way became the watchwords of vigilance for the whole school.

The syringe
I am the syringe
that you find in the street
A am the syringe
that attacks you on the waste ground

I am the syringe
that pricks you and kills you
I am the syringe
that you should stay away from!

I am like a live snake
that gives you a bite.
I am the live wire
that gives you a shock.
Stay away!
Or else you will have
a very short time to live!

What does it feel like
When you leave your child
Standing on the waste ground
and I prick her?
What would you do
when your child is infected?
What would you do?[9]

Sarah Weatherall

This was the living action of curriculum morality. Writing and reading for the benefit of your schoolmates; showing them vigilance, demonstrating the antidotes to pain and distress.

Yet the school's strongest moral position was in its defiance of the market. This stood at the centre of school policy. Inclusive and comprehensive, it invited and welcomed *all* students from all local communities and 'feeder' primary schools in its surrounding neighbourhoods—the advanced and less-advanced, the motivated and demotivated, those with every category of need. We stood as a school of the community—'for excellence and community' as we put below our letterhead. When children came to school hungry it offered them a free basic breakfast. When its community was threatened by the closure of the school, we stood up for ourselves as a vital community resource not only during our own official opening hours, but during the weekends and evenings when the school was used as an Arabic supplementary school, classes for Somali women, a Koranic school and extra classes run by graduates from the Yemeni community and the Pakistan Muslim Centre. We would not be closed, for closure—as parents and students and eventually the LEA realised— would be an act of sheer immorality. So we took the moral course and campaigned vigorously and successfully against closure, supported by our entire community. Students too, added their campaigning energies to the life and death struggle against closure and loss, for they also were fighting for what was right—their educational and cultural future and that of their families. Such a campaigning ethos was integral to the survival of the school. OFSTED called it 'politically unbalanced', yet it was right and necessary— anything else would have resulted in our demise at any point. Such campaigning became a democratic imperative for our students and their families. It meant participation, struggle, inter-communal dialogue and organisation for them, and through such expenditure of energy and thinking are gained understanding and meaning. Such an education is, at its foundation, deeply moral and devoted to the other human beings with whom you live, grow and share.

It is for these values and interpretations of right and wrong that this book was written and seeks to manifest—and the search and striving for their exemplification in action by students, teachers and communities. It was also for these same values that the régime, promoting them in the school—the governors and headteacher—were effectively barred and excluded from further leadership by the lords and bureaucrats of the system. But that is a narrative contained within the scope of what follows.

Notes

1 *The Times*, 31 October, 1996.
2 *Independent on Sunday*, 28 October, 1996.
3 *The Times*, 21 October, 1996.
4 Interview with Nigel de Gruchy, *Breakfast Time*, BBC1, 20 October, 1996
5 *Sunday Mirror*, 8 December, 1996.
6 *Daily Mirror*, 21 October, 1996.
7 *Morning Star*, 11 December, 1996.
8 Phillips, M., *All must have prizes*, London, 1996.
9 *Heart of Sheffield: Writings by students of Earl Marshal School*, Earl Marshal School, Sheffield, 1995.

A DIFFERENT ACHIEVEMENT: EXCELLENCE IN THE INNER CITY
(1996)

It happens during the last week of every August. As the national General Certificate of Secondary Education (GCSE) sixteen-plus examination results are announced, the local city newspapers are full of the success stories and photographs of glowing school students with their stratospheric grades— mostly those who attend suburban secondary schools. Some have gained ten or eleven subjects at the highest points of 'A' grade and the reports reflect their own and their parents' pride and praise. This is achievement, we are persuaded— its ultimate confirmation and popular expression, and as the government, step-by-step, re-shapes knowledge into the grim official plastic of its National Curriculum, continually tests young people on their inclination and ability to internalise and memorise, it then commissions OFSTED to police and enforce it, finally publishing its raw results in the form of school examination league tables— a new and deformed version of 'state education' begins to emerge.

This is not to decry or to devalue the huge effort and mental stamina that these young examinees have shown and proven, but it can only ever be just one part of the whole educational narrative. Maurice Bishop of Grenada, musing upon the frequent gulf between examination success and its usefulness in a speech on teacher education in the Caribbean, once observed that there were 'many certificated fools in the world'.[1] Such success needs to be measured within a much broader and many-sided exercise of experience and understanding, which breaks through and goes far beyond the walls of state-licensed and market-oriented knowledge and curriculum in a narrowly 'national' context. As poet of Tobago Eric Roach declared of democracy, so his words also speak of schools and education 'Be large, be critical!'[2]

But where are the inner city young people in all this rejoicing of examination success? Some are there too, and their achievement against all the social odds has been a truly formidable one. But the sky-high results are few and exceptional in the streets and estates on the other side of the city. This August, as with others, the celebrations are largely a middle class ritual.

What is achievement?

Yet here in our inner city school and in hundreds throughout Britain, every minute, every day there is an astonishing and continuous expression of achievement— a common achievement, a genius in the ordinary. Children of ten and younger have developed an ability to speak two languages fluently, moving in and out of each from one minute to the next as if they were switching existences. Thousands of teenagers who have lived in, studied in and absorbed into their brainpower and consciousness, into their very beings, two cultures, two nations, two peoples, two lives and who manage every day to cohere and order them, yet still move in and out of them as two separate worlds. The result is a control over living and use of language that the suburban child, with all his or her effective routines of study and examination proficiency, will know nothing of and be unable to penetrate. It is the difference between the assimilation of narrow fact and official knowledge as education—and the living of life as education. Which is the greater achievement? Yet which counts for all in the presently organised state system of education, and which counts for virtually nothing? That is the reality of the class distinction, cultural insult and permanent racism that is at the centre of the way achievement is recognised: the denial of the creative language reality and syncretic genius of hundreds of thousands of inner city young people, a reality of mass exclusion and institutional ignorance.

A Pakistani child who accompanies her mother to the DSS and translates into Punjabi for her, unravelling the massive social inequality within the complex bureaucratic word-maze of her second language, and bringing it into meaning and sometimes additional benefits for her mother: what a testing! Yet what reward or recognition, beyond a service of love— while a middle class child of the suburbs gets an 'A' in a 'modern language' like French or German, which she learns dutifully through books and teachers but rarely speaks or uses in any organic, life-centred way. While a Yemeni teenager spends his Saturdays and Sundays every week teaching Arabic to younger members of his community in the supplementary school organised, administered and staffed by volunteers in his community— what acknowledgement is there for him in the qualification powerhouse of the system? What accreditation? How will his expert and committed work help his entry into university? Yet rote-learning and swotting in the suburbs, endless phrases learned by heart and put down again on an 'A' level examination paper—and university is yours! So what is achievement: is it the banking of passive fact by an individual learner, or the use and application of living experience in the service of others and the struggle to develop your own community?

Yet such living achievement has often reached a long way down a journey for the inner city student: the young man or woman who has arrived— sometimes having tramped across the scrubland of northern Somalia to cross a frontier and reach refuge from war—and those who have gone back in order to go further in their lives. Here a boy speaks of his coming, from a village in the mountains of southern Yemen:

> Yesterday we had packed up everything. All our relatives were at our house, they were wishing us good luck. People like my Grandma and Auntie were crying because they couldn't bear to see us go. My Mum was really upset and worried at having to leave her family. Me and my brother enjoyed playing

with our friends in the sand, but they knew that we were leaving. I felt nervous
and very excited about what to expect to find and do in England.

My Grandma would say to us, 'Where is this country, England?'

I told her, 'Oh, it is an island, very far away.' And my Grandmother said,
'what kind of country floats in water?'

I explained to my Grandma about it. She didn't understand, but I knew
that she only asked these questions because she was deeply upset at having
to say goodbye to us. I also knew that I would miss my Grandma and friends.
I knew I would be quite lonely as there was only my Dad who I knew in
England.

Then the arrival in England, a time for the fusion of reconciliation and strangeness:

Then for the first time in three years I saw my Dad. He was waiting for us
and I ran towards him and hugged him. He kissed me and then kissed my
brother Nageeb. He gave us sweets and fruits. The sweets I didn't even
recognise and they were not like I had tasted before. And I ate an apple and
a banana, then my Dad took us to the taxi.

The people in England seemed really strange and different. They talked in
a language that made me feel lonely as I could not understand what they
were saying. My Mum found it really good and easy to cook and get the food,
but she was very lonely as my Dad was working in the factory. She had no
one to talk to but us. Then after a few weeks another Arab family moved into
the neighbourhood and my Mum became good friends with that woman, and
that took her mind off her mother and family.[3]

There is a lifetime of childhood here: an exchange of nations and peoples and the
grasp of a deep learning experience at such an early age. The same is true for the child
who returns. She finds a life and a country she had not expected under the myths that
her new consciousness itself uncovers. It is an education of the mind and heart— as
George Lamming wrote, 'to make the mind feel ... and to make the feeling think.'[4] That
is the process that thousands of inner city young people explore on journeys to and
sojourns within the lands of their parents. For it is an affirmation found in a country
which is now theirs too:

When I finally arrived in Yemen I was surprised at what I saw because I
had imagined it like a great dump with snakes and insects everywhere you
looked. My first impressions were beautiful as I felt the hot air hit my face. In
the beginning I felt uncomfortable because I felt that people were staring at
me, but my parents told me not to worry because I was surrounded by family
and friends.

When I got home to my part of the city, I felt at home. I heard the *ethane*
(the man in the mosque) calling for the people to pray. When I first heard this
my heart skipped a beat. The man's voice really touched me and the things he

was saying really made me feel at home. I *felt* like a proper muslim, even though I am one.

I felt free and happy all the time. The view from my bedroom window was enough to last me a lifetime. I could see the buildings. They were very different, high with lots of windows and I could see the blue sky and the green sea and the palm trees surrounding the mosque.

The first day we went out to the market and my father bought us some fruit. I was so surprised at the beauty of the fruit that it was enough to fill my eyes. The people surrounding me were very friendly and I felt equal because I was at home.

Yemen is not a very rich country but I was surprised at how it had built itself up over the previous years. Women in Aden were so free that they could do whatever they wished, but I had to wear a headscarf and an *abaya*, which is like a long cloak.

One day me and my sister went to a friend's house. Her name was Safa. She took us to the beach and we walked up and down the sand— it was beautiful. There were so many things to do in so little time.

Five weeks later my three sisters got married to my mum's brother's sons. It was a triple wedding and Arabic weddings last five days. On the first day you wear casual clothes and on the second you wear green. On the third day you wear any colour that you wish and on the fourth you may wear any colour again. Yet these four days were the worst that I had ever known, knowing that I had to go back to Britain without my sisters.

On the last day of the wedding, my sisters went home. It was the worst day of my life, it was as if someone had taken a piece of my heart.

Two weeks later we had to come back to Britain. We all said our goodbyes and since that day I arrived, I have never felt the same about that country again.

The achievement behind this story is not only to have travelled and been there, but it is also to have opened yourself to the other, to know another life and to allow it to change you and become a part of you. It is living as learning: learning as living. That is education, and that is the experience of many inner city young people that is largely unacknowledged in the formal state system. So much so, that such journeys and sojourns, when they take place in school time, which is usually inevitable, are deemed to be nothing more then 'interruptions' to the conventional school curriculum and judged negatively. They are, however, often the most vibrant and revealing learning experiences in a young person's life and need to be recognised, accredited and built upon not only within family and community, but with a strong sense of value in school too. For the 'community school' must never be a narrow or parochial concept, but a school of the world. It is a base for affirming and extending the internationalism of its very nature and commitment. Its curriculum, quite simply, is not of one 'nation' but of all nations;

not of a single British people but of all life and peoples— the unifying of cultures and nature as a power for development, justice and beauty.

Or there is the fourteen year old Pakistani girl who journeys to the centre of her family's faith and yearns to share the depth of her experience with all whom she knows— and the whole world, if possible. As she prepares to leave for Mecca with her uncle, her aunt and grandmother start to cry: 'Me and my uncle laughed at them and said, 'we're not going to World War Three, we're going to a fabulous place! Coming in to land over the city, she sees below 'the wonderful lights of Mecca' and is astonished by their beauty. Then when she visits the great Mosque she 'couldn't stop looking at it. I mean it was so beautifully clean and neat. It was shining from all over, and half of it was made of real gold.' The huge oneness of a whole community at prayer moves her deeply, but she suddenly comes back to a real world:

> When we prayed, all the world in Saudi Arabia is at the Mosque. We prayed, and before you pray you clean yourself, you wash your arms, face and feet. Suddenly in the place where the women were cleaning themselves the lights went off, and when they came back on again after about five minutes I looked in the sink. There were grasshoppers and lizards. I screamed. It was a very big sink— the taps just went on and on to God knows where. At least a hundred people can wash themselves there.

She endures the burning heat: 'After we came back from the Mosque, we had a bath and got ready for the five very hard days in the tents. Believe me, it is so, so hot. It seems the sun's on the floor.' As she makes her last visit to the Mosque, the mundane and the mystical seem to jell:

> We came back to make our last visit to the Mosque, to say hello to the black stone. We were very, very thirsty. We all started to cry: 'Our Prophet's in heaven and the devil's in hell!' It was all like a dream. It was absolutely amazing.

I'd love to go again, and I hope that every human being goes there.

Deficit and deprivation

How can this knowledge and experience be set down as 'deprivation' or 'disadvantage'? Yet the deficit approach to inner city education, the portrayal of students and parents in terms of problems after problems, only increases the burden on their breaking out from the caricatures heaped upon them. For their achievement is measured by the ever-narrowing official curriculum, becoming more and more impositional under the control of Conservative educators and ideologues such as Dr. Tate and his preoccupations with national identity and the vindication through history of truly 'British' heroes[5]— and overseen by the formulaic inspection criteria and processes of the OFSTED network. Authentic working class and internationalist inner city experience is squeezed and excluded, with the imagination and energies fusing learning with life and human freedom being pressed tighter and tighter by every new proclaimed 'order' from SEAC and the new masters of officialised curriculum development. Thereby, living achievement becomes 'underachievement', bilingualism or a fluency in Arabic, Punjabi, Somali or Bengali becomes either irrelevant or an expression of linguistiç poverty— and the immersion in cultures other than a white British norm or a European language becomes a degeneration into cultural 'disadvantage'. If we accept or work within the terminal dimensions of these definitions, the achievement of the majority of inner city children will never be equitably recognised or accredited. Instead, we should be raising the value-laden criteria of their own communities' aspirations in education, campaigning for the achievement of bilingualism in the inner city to be understood and accredited as the equivalent of one 'A' level for university entry, or for the consistent participation in the teaching and organisation of community supplementary or language schools and classes to be recognised formally as deserving another 'A' level in Community Development. Universities too, and those who frame their admission policies, need to be at the centre of this process, working closely alongside inner city schools and communities. Thus we would be promoting and campaigning around criteria that genuinely affirm and develop the cultural strength and achievements in the lives of many thousands of inner city young people, and struggling to open university doors to their commitment and talent.

The Damage of the Act

The force and alienation of government persuasion following the enactment of the 1988 Education Act has already wrought much damage and confusion to education and schools in the inner cities. While the well-resourced, prestigious suburban schools appear to offer their students a straight road to 'A' levels and university entry, the government uses them, through its 'open enrolment' policy, to entice inner city parents to abandon schools close to home. This was a move also symbolically undertaken by the leader of the 'Opposition' Labour Party, Tony Blair, who enrolled his own son in a grant-maintained school, well-traditioned and well streamed, at some distance from his Islington home.

The 1993 case of the inner city, mainly Bangladeshi, parents who went to court against Bradford City Council, accusing it of racism by allocating their children to local schools rather than allowing them free entry into, as the *Yorkshire Post*[6] put it, the 'best upper schools located in the Aire Valley', shows how convincing has been the government attack on inner city schools. The *Times Educational Supplement* put the argument and the myth pithily: 'White middle class schools offer the best route out of the underclass for poor Asian kids and parents actually have a choice.' In fact, the reality of government strategy is to increasingly present no choice, as local schools are gradually bled dry and closed down— with suburban *schools* presented with the right to choose rather than working class *parents*. Furthermore, the number of inner city children who are sentenced to long-distance education far from their friends and communities, who are disenchanted by and opting out of suburban schools and transferring back to schools in their local neighbourhoods— is also an observable phenomenon. As the Bradford Labour councillor, Malcolm Waters, concluded after the case of racism against the local council was turned down by the High Court in September 1993: 'We have sympathy with every parent who may have believed that government policy guaranteed their right to the school of their choice, but it does not.' This choice is a phantom one and a part of the duplicity of the 1988 Act. Yet while the Bradford Parents' case of the blatant discrimination suffered by those communities living in geographically and economically-defined struggling areas of the inner city was undoubtedly true, nowhere in the establishment press could be found a defence or advocacy of inner city schools, or their potential in offering local communities a democratic and achievement-founded alternative to the estranged and faraway education of suburban schools.

Unlimited ambition

Far from the convenient myths hatched about inner city children being bereft of aspiration and desire to succeed in education, ask our students what their ambitions are— there is no limit to them. These have often come with their parents, travelling oceans and continents to strive to make them real. The school's major daily task is to help to achieve and realise them, and passing examinations in conventional school terms and National Curriculum terms is of vital importance for inner city young people. Yet their teachers have so much more to do too, putting this official knowledge into a critical framework and offering alternative perspectives, broadening and internationalising curriculum and developing work against racism and sexism, creating new forums and activities within the community and democratic structures and practices within the school, stimulating learning and pride in black and working class history and culture, transforming individualised and capsulised notions of knowledge, value and experience so that our students can see in their future an ambition not only for themselves, but for their communities too.

A Pakistani boy says: 'My ambition is to be a doctor, a casualty doctor because I want to save lives and help sick people. I'm not going to be a lazy one like some doctors that only do it for money. I'm going to do my best to help people.' A girl classmate adds: 'My ambition is to be a nursery teacher because I'd like to teach children all I can. I care about children's education ... I would like to go to Pakistan and other countries and teach the children there about all kinds of subjects.' Another girl writes: 'I want to be a doctor because I want to save people to live and be proud of myself. I would like to help the Bosnian people because they are dying and I want them to live longer and enjoy their lives. I want to be part of a big group to help them because I don't want them to be fighting all their lives.' Another knows the real situation in Pakistan, for he writes, 'you have to pay to go to the Doctor's there and it is a lot of money. I want to be a doctor to help those who can't afford to go.' Rizwana tells of her lifetime's hope: 'Ever since I was small my ambition was to be a teacher. I would like very much to be a nursery teacher because I like small children and I think that nursery education is important before you start school.'

Then there is Fatima, twelve years old and writing defiantly:

> My ambition is to be a lawyer who takes cases and fights for justice in the court. I would like to be a lawyer because I want to fight for justice and the rights of people. Also I don't want guilty people freed and innocent people jailed. I would like to help people get their rights, not jailed for what they haven't done. I would like to give people the courage to speak in the court, and not be frightened.

These are not lives and futures seen from a deficit vision, rather from a clarity and determination to see success and fulfilment personally, and for others and whole communities too. Neither is there ambiguity about achievement and what it means. It is bonded with service, internationalism and love for ordinary people on two continents and across the world. It is upon this strength of *community* and aspiration that we, as teachers, need to build our work in the schools of the inner cities, within a culture which now goes beyond points 'national' and expresses the world. This culture needs also to be in the hearts of our schools and those who practice a critical pedagogy within a dialogue of the classroom, standing up against the passive notion that teachers are simply 'deliverers' of a formulaic and prefabricated curriculum handed down to them. Such an education can only be moribund and demotivating. Instead, teachers must live up to their true mission as active makers of curriculum in collaboration with their students, keeping knowledge and achievement alive and in perpetual process and creating schools which are true meeting places of curriculum and community.

References

1   See 'Education is a Must!' in Searle, Chris, (Ed.) *In Nobody's Backyard: Maurice Bishop's Speeches*, 1979-1983, Zed Books, London 1984.

2   From 'Caribbean Coronation Verse', *The Flowering Rock: Collected Poems of E. M. Roach*, Peepal Tree Press, Leeds 1993

3   This quotation, and those following, are from *School of the World*, Earl Marshal School, Sheffield 1994.

4   'A Visit to Carriacou' from Lamming, George, *Conversations: Essays, Addresses and Interviews, 1953-1990*, Karia Press, London 1992.

5   See article 'Britain's heroes find a champion in the English Classroom' by MacLeod, Donald, *Guardian*, 19 September 1995

6   *Yorkshire Post*, 11 September 1993

7   *Times Educational Supplement*, 17 September 1993

LIVING COMMUNITY, LIVING SCHOOL (1992)

The Chilean national poet, Pablo Neruda, once wrote that 'a crowd is made into a people through duty and love.' Beyond all the use and abuse of the word 'community' over the years, we could add to that statement, 'a group is made into a community by unity and struggle.'

There have been so many variants of the notion of a 'community school' through the history of education, that we need to know, very clearly, what we mean by this 'community' that is served by the school we are striving to create. And in tackling this process of definition I find myself asking again, and carrying around inside me as a teacher, the question asked of me once by a Pakistani colleague, who, I believe, was paraphrasing some of the words of the Prophet when he put to me, 'Are you talking about the school which is at the heart of the community, or do you mean a school which has the community in its heart?'

He and I were both talking about a particular community in the city of Sheffield in England, but a community which has its distinct similarities—despite its special differences—to others in many cities in Britain, Europe and North America. And in recognising difference, I want to concentrate upon specifics which create similarity, and give the idea of 'community' in inner-city education some kind of generic meaning.

From the same class

First and foremost, this community sprang from the working class experience, and a great manufacturing industry: steel making. It also remembers the proud hallmarks 'Made in Sheffield' which marked the cutlery of the world that was produced in this city. As one eleven year old boy was told by his grandfather:

> My Grandad said Sheffield wer' proud
> And its cutlery works wer' well known.
> It made knives and forks by the thousand
> And sent them all over the globe.[1]
>
> Rupert (11)

Other young people have also had such memories passed on to them through their families:

> From one end to the other of the River Don,
> Steelworks stood together
> Where the work was done.
> Though every brick was shaken

> At the clanging of the hammers
> No notice could be taken
> Of the never-ending clamour.
> Chimneys belched out dirt and smoke -
> Yellow, brown and grimy black.
> Work trains carried steel and coke
> From the works and back.
> Steam sirens screamed their raucous blasts
> At six and ten and two.
> Workers hurried thick and fast,
> By factory gates they queued.
>
> Andrea (15)

Yet now this has gone and such images are 'false dreams' for the young people of the city that bring them no jobs. The true picture for them around the north east of Sheffield is very different:

> Steel forges are silent
> Not even death tolls knell,
> No workers troop the factory gates
> At the sound of work-end bell.
> Once a throbbing heartline,
> The steelworker's dream,
> Now a decadent rust-site
> Where no life can be seen.
>
> Philip (15)

or

> Rain now falls on the empty scene
> Rusting the hammers until they bleed,
> Forming red rivers
> Of misery and pain.
>
> Julian (15)

And as the 'steel city' lies demolished, over its ruins come new and less substantial foundations:

> Bright new shopping centres begin to appear,
> But angry Sheffield people look on with fear.
>
> Robert (15)

These young people know very well, and write in their poetry that 'dying cities' have 'no fiscal miracles to bring', as the manufacturing industry of their parents' and grandparents' years has gone with the steel. They have few illusions, and look starkly at the future. But one prospect which they do see is a glimpse of a new, future community. An eleven year old Bengali girl can see it and begin to conceptualise it in very concrete terms:

> Young people new people
> And old people live there.
> Put together,
> Making a new community.
>
> Mispha (11)

And these people 'put together' through history, from many parts of the world, have now decided by choice and circumstance to stay, and live here. Some, certainly even by constraint and default, but others through much more positive energies, even when they may have other and very different places to consider:

> I was born in Sheffield from a baby girl.
> Sheffield is my home and my part of the world ...
> I'm a Yemeni but I'm also a Sheffielder,
>
> I love Yemen but I also love it here.
>
> Munitta (15)

Such feelings prompt the urge to re-make a city, and put powerful choices before the lives of its young people:

> Sheffield lies in our hands, in our hands it lies.
> We can get out and do something
> Or watch it while it dies.
>
> John (11)

But the willpower and stamina needed to face up to the consequences of a positive choice takes this new community towards having to unite, and having to struggle:

> People who may have no home
> No place to go, no way to turn,
> This is our city now, maybe forever,
> We've got to fight and stay together.
>
> Katie (15)

Communities and struggle

I have quoted these young people's words at length, not only because they carry such truth and a grounding optimism but because they express the four principles that I have to make about my use of the word 'community'. They are belongingness, organisation, unity and struggle. These principles need to be understood within the context of an inner-city, working class population composed of people of a number of national origins who have had very different sets of life experiences and continue to live their lives often in separate cultural and religious ways. But for all these peoples *education* has remained all-important. It was to find work for themselves and education and a secure future for their children that they came to Sheffield. For those—often of the next generation—whose hopes for a successful education ended in a school system failing them, has grown an even stronger determination that such an outcome will never be re-visited upon their own children when their turn comes. Education, and more specifically the schools that their children go to stay at the heart of their lives and hopes for any new community and can become a special catalyst for making a genuine cohesion. Of course, issues of education and in particular parental choice of schools, can also be among the most divisive questions in any such community, driving wedges between individuals and groups as they may contest for admission to the 'best' schools in parts of the city miles away from where they live and pour scorn upon the 'second-rate' local schools within their own neighbourhoods. It is such attitudes and the volatile social and political doubts and misconceptions which they create, that the Baker legislation has sought to inflame and capitalise upon, usually to the damage of local schools.

Yet, as so often happens, campaigns waged and benefits won by black people in local working class communities are soon felt by working class people generally, as the advantages accrue to all who use the resources involved. In such struggles, education has often provided a prominent battlefield. This process was signalled in 1970 over the controversy surrounding the disproportionate number of Afro-Caribbean children being placed by local education authorities in schools for so-called 'educationally sub-normal' (ESN) children. The inner-city Caribbean communities—particularly those in North London—waged a strong and well-organised campaign around this issue, which was made more effective by a potent pamphlet written by one of the campaign activists, Bernard Coard: *How the West Indian Child is made educationally sub-normal in the British school system.*[2] The victory of this campaign was truly pathfinding. A precedent of educational struggle was created by a black community, which raised an entire education system's consciousness over the negative and very damaging 'labelling' of black children as they journeyed through their school lives. 'ESN' schools were abolished in name (although other sinister names have often been used to replace them) and thousands of white children and their families also benefited from this. But the important difference now is that Caribbean communities have become vigilant, combative and campaign-conscious in their understanding that never again will they allow their children to be so collectively derided and blatantly mis-categorised. In 1985, when Caribbean parents launched another campaign in a number of British cities—this time against their children suffering a disproportionate amount of suspensions, exclusions and expulsions from school — the lessons of the anti-ESN campaign a decade and a half before were there to inform and inspire them.

Reporting that black children in general were six times more likely to be suspended from schools than other pupils, the *Caribbean Times* of 14 March 1985 commented in its editorial:

> But with an increasing number of black pupils unjustifiably siphoned off into so-called special units and many others suffering suspension or expulsion for relatively minor incidents in schools, it is now clear that public awareness of racism within schools must be heightened. Black parents will also step up their fight against their children's education suffering because of harsh and excessive punishments. In short, black parents, as they have shown in Nottingham, Reading, Bristol and Brent, will not tolerate their children being pushed to the educational margins.
>
> There will be no further tolerance of black schoolchildren being unfairly thrown out of school just prior to their preparations for examinations. Black parents, as reports from the aforementioned areas show, have seen too many of their children scuttled out of schools onto the streets where the police are waiting to pick them up and begin the criminalising process.Local education authorities can expect to bear the brunt of further protests until they take decisive action

Indeed they had to. In Sheffield for example, the Caribbean community association pressurised the Education Department to organise a 'survey' of suspensions and exclusions in all its schools. When this exercise proved clearly that black students (as well as working class students) were suffering disproportionately through these procedures, the Caribbean community successfully campaigned—alongside other black communities—for a special educational initiative involving the establishing of over a hundred new posts that would serve all Sheffield's black communities.

This tradition of struggle for educational betterment has been built by inner-city black communities from the power and effectiveness of their organisations. There is a direct correlation between the successful outcomes of campaigns which the communities have waged and the strength of their community organisations. Sheffield's Caribbean community has Sheffield and District Afro-Caribbean Association (SADACCA) which has based and given consolidation to its frequent educational campaigns, offering a venue for meetings, administrative and clerical support, a centre for discussion and social life, and a means of linking education struggles with other campaigns, interventions and developmental work around issues of housing, health, employment, culture and general economic advancement.

The experience of Sheffield's Yemenis

Much the same is true for Sheffield's Yemeni Community Association which, as well as organising and coordinating struggles and campaigns which the Yemenis mounted around compensation for redundancy and industrial deafness relating to the collapse of the steel industry—where the majority of the male workforce had found employment upon arrival from Yemen in the fifties and sixties—was in the forefront of developing community education initiatives. The situation was complicated by there being two separate Yemeni states and two community organisations in Sheffield serving Yemenis of different national origins. But there was always cooperation between them during struggles for community progress—which was why when unification was achieved between the two Yemens in 1990, it was greeted with such relief and happiness by the Sheffield Yemenis. For now they could carry forward their own unity too, which had been developing for many years. But the development of community organisations and literacy and re-training initiatives moved as parallel developments after the community suffered such large scale redundancies with the collapse of the steel industry in the early eighties. As Abdulgalil Shaif, a community organiser, reflected:

> Circumstances were indeed grim. Unemployment raised issues which weren't there before, issues of loneliness, isolation and depression. People found themselves walking the streets, sitting in cafes, playing cards, unable to retrain because of lack of opportunities, language difficulties and illiteracy which has always been one of the biggest problems that the community has faced. Of course, if there had been this retraining or the existence of literacy classes, it would have helped in the creation of alternatives, or of a new direction for the community, but there was nothing for our people. For the Yemenis there were no opportunities, no encouragement or understanding for a new and changed future to suit their needs. So the Yemeni community organisations, as they exist now, were born out of those very real and concrete problems.[3]

As the young people of the community also struggled against low expectations and underachievement within the school system, their families realised they needed its organisations to make interventions there too—and to set up alternatives and supplementary education projects. Shaif (who was later to gain, a doctorate at Sheffield University) remembers his own schooling as representative of what many Yemeni school students — as well as those from other black and working class families — were led to experience. As he concluded the only antidote was resistance, both individual and organisational:

> The young Yemenis were born into black working class families. They could easily have followed in the same footsteps as their parents. Their lives at school were to experience racism, to find failure and reach a standard of education that was unacceptable to both themselves and their parents. There wasn't that encouragement or opportunity. We can't look back and say that the school system served us well. For example, I was advised by my headteacher and

other teachers to go on the Youth Training Scheme. But I was adamant. I
wanted to take A levels. But they told me my CSE's weren't good enough. It
was a chronic system of low expectations for black and working class children.
But I *knew* that with encouragement and opportunity I could do well. Even
though I knew that when they looked at me they could only see failure, without
seeing or understanding my potential. That was typical, and it is still happening.
I knew that if I went on YTS I would end up with the same kind of life and
prospects as my father. And I also knew that he didn't come all the way from
Yemen to Sheffield for that to happen.

For the adults, the issue of literacy became even more crucial as they searched for
new employment. The local education authority and official structures were offering
nothing. The community had to take the lead.

During the early seventies we had organised in an ad-hoc manner literacy
classes in Arabic, run by volunteers. Otherwise there was very little educational
activity. The first issue we identified in the late seventies was the need to
continue, strengthen and develop this literacy work within the community.
This was taken very seriously, and was organised without any help or funding
from the local education authority. The thinking was that if people learned
Arabic they would be able to read newspapers from back home, write letters
and keep in close contact with events and families in the Yemen. They would
be able to pass on the Arabic language to their children—and this was seen
as essential. It was always feared that our children would grow up without
their language: and without their language, without their culture and identity.
Others saw it for different reasons. For example, my father urged me to learn
Arabic so I could explain to him in Arabic what was happening in Britain and
how to work the British system of life. He took me with him to the DHSS, he
took me with him to the Tax Office, even to the firm to get his wages. He took
me with him because he thought that someone would say something to him
that he couldn't understand. So we were there as interpreters, as translators,
as a support mechanism to our parents. The parents felt proud and secure,
having a bilingual child with them.

So the first community language schools developed in the late seventies.
They developed in the context of a disinterest and discouragement from the
local school system. They ignored our needs. I went to several schools to ask
for support and to use their resources to open a community language class,
and they said 'No. If you want to open a class somewhere, go ahead, it's up to
you but we're not taking any notice of this.' I don't know whether it was the
schools seeing these classes as competing with them, or whether they frowned
on them because they were classes being run and provided by 'unprofessional'
people. But whatever their reasons, the assumptions were racist, that we
couldn't run these classes properly, that they were unnecessary, or that these

Yemenis are running their own classes today, tomorrow they might open a factory next door! Those sort of stereotypes flourished. The schools didn't see us as a part of the community that is enriching their school. But we saw it that way—that if the children learned their own community's language, they would bring that bilingualism as a benefit into the mainstream of school life and culture. They would develop much more quickly and deeply at school, and then be able to transmit their concepts and ideas in a much fuller way, thus improving and broadening what was going on at school. I came through a community language school, and the ideas and skills it sparked with me I passed on to my younger brother and sisters in Arabic, to my cousins in Arabic, to my parents in Arabic, and the whole community has learned from them. If I had been educated in English only, I could never have transferred these things in this way, and they would have been isolated within me and the community would not have benefited. You see, we think education is about sharing, cooperating, learning from each other, passing on insights and exchanging thoughts, developing our community—we need our languages if we are going to do that.

Our first language school started in a hut in a park in Crookes, that we shared with the Caribbean community. It was the first example of cooperation between our two communities. It would take about forty to fifty children. It was far too small and the children would spill out into the park, and we had to teach them there. It was our first feeling of the struggle shared by both communities—they were speaking in Creole and we were learning Arabic. Unfortunately this cooperation didn't develop — I wished it had done — but these are the kind of shared experiences which we need to discuss and learn from in the future.

Then in 1985 the Yemeni Community Association began. There had been a change in the receptivity and sensitivity within the Sheffield City Council. They had started listening to us at last, and this was a very important development as it resulted in some funding for and the renovation of this building that we are sitting in now. It was also an important development for the host community, the white community as they recognised us as a community, with specific needs and features. Before that it was as if they had never seen us, we were an invisible community, to them. They didn't realise that Yemenis living here saw Sheffield as their home. It was our home also. We may have had a family and a home in Yemen, but we loved Sheffield too. I, like all Yemenis here, am proud to know this as my home. When I am at home in Yemen I think of my home in Sheffield. It may be two homes, but so what? We're proud of that. If I can improve links between my home in Yemen and my home in Sheffield, I would love to. If I could help local white people go to Yemen, I'd love to, that's the beauty of it. I support anything that benefits ordinary people in this country, as well as in, Yemen, whether it's the development of their community, their education housing, health and all other opportunities, then, I support it. I support the development between Britain and all Third World countries. This why the "Cricket Test" idea of only supporting one particular people or group that Norman Tebbit came out with would be unbelievable for me and all Yemenis. When I'm in Yemen I miss Sheffield, I want to come back to Sheffield so much. Yet when I'm here I long for returning to Yemen, particularly now as it is united at last.

Then two years ago we developed our Yemeni Literacy Campaign. We had studied, and been inspired by the literacy campaign in the south of Yemen in the years following independence, which was very successful. Our campaign here in Sheffield came about through a collaborative approach both from inside the community, and sincere people inside the education system. It was a combined struggle by the older people who wanted literacy, the younger people who wanted further education and careers, and workers and administrators in education who were prepared to fight for resources for black communities.

These three elements were linked and organised together. Already we have had sixty to seventy people involved and out of these twenty to thirty per cent have gone onto courses in further education, and others to various employment schemes. It has also radicalised a community that has always been culturally bound — especially its women. The Yemeni community has always been politically forward — particularly in its consciousness of being working class and internationalist, in its support for the Miners' Strike, for example, or for the Palestinians or the struggle against Apartheid as well as its solidarity with the Yemen Revolution and the anti-colonial and anti-imperialist struggle. But we always had cultural issues that sometimes held us back and needed to be tackled, and the literacy campaign came at the right time to help us tackle them. It brought our young women to the forefront of the community. The school system had failed our young women too. It had never reached out to them or their parents and built links with the communities and families to try to understand them, or encourage them, to identify the ways in which they were culturally restricted, or to give advice or offer career development that could push their daughters towards new paths in life. My younger sister wanted to be a doctor, but if I had not been around to help and encourage her she would never have moved towards that aspiration. The school would not have done it. But I am certain that she will be a doctor, she has all the attributes — the intelligence, the determination and the patience.

Now the literacy campaign has brought the parents of the young people right into the heart of education. They are being educated by their own sons and daughters. The family and the community have become *one* in this campaign, the youngers and the elders. And the parents have no seen that the young people have the ability to teach and the young people have recognised this in themselves. So in a few years time they can become qualified and come into the state schools as teachers, or take up other professional careers like doctors or lawyers and eventually give service back to the community. All these possibilities are visible to them now. And what has been most radical is that the young women involved in the campaign as literacy assistants have been the most dynamic and successful elements. This has helped to remove the stereotype of passivity attached to our women from both within and outside the community.

All these advances won by the Yemeni community have come within the context of *organising* around issues of education. It is important evidence stressing the links between education and community development, and how local schools can play either a positive or entirely unhelpful role in that process.

'Communities of resistance'

The Sheffield Bangladeshis too—like the Yemenis they had been a part of the low-paid, unskilled workforce who did the jobs white workers rejected during the latter days of the Sheffield steel industry—experienced similar struggles but with a different emphasis. In the seventies and early eighties, their children—many of them newcomers, who, with their mothers were joining their fathers in Britain, experienced some of the same street-level violence and hostility faced by Bangladeshis of East London during the same period. Not only were they targets as they travelled to and from a secondary school next to a large and run-down white estate which was some distance out of the neighbourhood where they lived, but once there they found themselves separated and isolated in the 'language centre' attached to the school. The community, through its organisation, the Bangladesh Welfare Association (which had grown out of the East Pakistan Welfare Association after independence), had to take on this combination of racist violence and racist quarantining:

> Our children were going to the local school and met a different dimension of racism there. They were going to 'language centres', trying to acquire skills in English and then moving on to mainstream schooling. But within this process they had to experience racist abuse and physical attack, very often violent. The police were involved and very often serious fights took place immediately outside the school perimeter. Our children were bussed in and out of the school for a long time.[4]

Yet while they struggled they also built, and continually badgered the largely disinterested local education authority for support and resources. Like the Yemenis and their Arabic schools the voluntary, self-organised Bengali language classes after formal school hours in the premises of the local infants schools brought the community closer together and consolidated its organisation. And like the Yemenis too, and their efforts to emulate in Sheffield the successes of the literacy campaign mounted in their homeland, the Bangladeshis took inspiration from the huge commitment of their people in their country of origin to their national language. This loyalty went back to the pre-independence period when West Pakistan had imposed its own language, Urdu, on the Bengali-speaking people of the eastern enclave. On 21 February 1952 at a protest march called by the movement campaigning for Bengali to have equal status as a national language with Urdu many Bengalis were shot down and killed in the streets of Dacca. As Mahmood Rahman, a local Bengali teacher, described the impact of that massacre, its effects can be clearly seen in the Bengali mother tongue classes organised by the community in Sheffield:

> Above all, this was the day we really grew to know ourselves. The roots of our nationhood were discovered on this day through our proud assertion to the right of our own language. We have never forgotten this and will never forget it, no matter where we are, no matter where our lives take us.
>
> Our whole struggle then became a struggle to establish a proper and respected status for our language.[5]

With such massive determination and emotion behind ensuring that these Bengali classes grew and consolidated for the young people of the community, the local education authority began at last to offer some belated recognition:

> Our mother tongue classes created broader opportunities not only for our young people, but for our adults too. The local education authority began to take note of these developments. We were the pioneers in the city in initiating these classes.

And as is the way with pioneers the Bangladeshis opened up LEA recognition for the mother tongue classes of other black communities across the city.

The educational activity helped stimulate the mounting of other campaigns such as those around divided families and the reuniting of fathers with mothers and children still in Bangladesh, for better trade union representation, for housing improvements, for support for Bangladesh itself and its people beleaguered by climatic disasters, for jobs and retraining. Again, the collective confidence of a community had been strengthened around its struggles for education.

For Sheffield's Somalis education has become even more of a vital lifeline. There has been a small community of Somalis from the northern regions of the country in Sheffield since shortly after the end of the Second World War, when Somali men came to Britain without their families to work as labourers in the steel industry. After using up much of their wages for many years in visits home, their families started joining them twenty years ago and a new black community was established. This has grown substantially since the outbreak of civil war in northern Somalia in 1988 and the genocidal purges by the military forces of Siad Barré and his government against the peoples of cities such as Hargeisa and Burao. Refugee families have arrived directly from this conflict and via refugee camps in eastern Ethiopia, with their children having witnessed and lived through years of horror and trauma. Their suffering is much greater knowing that their houses, their schools and hospitals — together with the entire infrastructure of their society, have been completely destroyed.

For the arrivant Somalis, community organization in Sheffield has meant survival, and education into the language and ways of England had to be an integral part of that. As the number of Somali refugee families increased, the community experienced a tense period with government and local council departments, whose bureaucracies seemed at an impasse to help them. Ibrahim Gure, a teacher, recounted

> The Department of Social Security (DSS) refused to give community care grants to some refugees claiming they were not eligible. There were other complaints about the Housing Department giving large families small, unsuitable accommodation.[6]

As they did not qualify for language teaching resources under Section 11 of the Local Government Act (which only applies to people from the 'New Commonwealth and Pakistan'), Somali children struggled in schools with no Somali language support and no English as a Second Language teaching. College students, because of their asylum-seeking status, were not given grants to allow them to follow essential English and training courses to be able to find employment. Again, education became one of the signal issues with which the Somali Community Association had to grapple. And through all these struggles the community had to deal with central government harassment and hostile legislation as racist feeling was being stoked up against genuine refugees, asylum-seekers and a new generation of black people entering Britain—with the tabloid press adding its full assistance to prejudice and rejection. Huge, degrading, front page banner headlines suggesting that refugees from Africa are likely to be rapists or frauds in newspapers like the *Daily Mail*[7], voicing their alarm at "the flood of asylum seekers' or quoting police officers saying that 'many immigrants come here for an easy life because we are an easy touch', make life in inner-city Britain no easier for the Somali newcomers—who are already striving in an unknown language to deal with the effects of poverty, poor or no housing, unemployment and the continuing pain of the war they have left behind.

For the rural Pakistanis who came to Sheffield from the districts of Mirpur and Kashmir during the sixties and seventies, education was a precious premium. Their families had rarely known it in a formal sense, and it had been a rare and bold—as well as expensive—decision of one of the parents that had propelled a son towards school. As one Pakistani retired worker remembered from his house in Sheffield.

I was born in a very remote village where donkeys were the main form of transportation and buying bricks to build a house was out of people's reach entirely. There was no significance or importance given to education. If an odd one or two studied, it was only up to primary level. Beyond that, education was considered as a Hindu's job because they were involved in business. We were peasants and toiled as labourers day and night worrying about not having enough to eat.

When I was five years old my late mother, breaking with the family tradition, enrolled me in a primary school. At home it became a point of discussion and the question was constantly asked, 'Why should he be sent to school to bear the brunt of the schoolmaster's caning?" No one on my father's side or my mother's side had ever been to school. Everybody went against my mother's decision, but my mother had only one desire in life—that I should study up to matriculation and become an officer, or at least a clerk. I was five years old; not only had I to walk four miles each way to school but I also had to carry my satchel with books in. Usually I carried it on my head.[8]

But the experience of emigration and the need to prosper in a British inner-city has created many more Pakistani mothers and fathers who aspire for their children and wish so deeply for their success and deliverance from the lack of schooling they knew themselves. Like the father who arrived in Sheffield as an itinerant worker who had carried bricks in Mirpur, became a servant to an aristocratic family in Lahore, had returned to his family land in Kashmir, had been a dock-worker and cotton factory hand in Karachi, a sackmaker in Southampton, a railway track-maker in Dewsbury, a dishwasher in Indian restaurants in London, a cutlery worker in Rochdale and Sheffield and eventually a self-employed milkman in a neighbourhood in the north-east of the Steel City, his advice to his son, (set down in the son's account of his father's working life) reflects the importance he puts upon his children grasping hold of the opportunity for education that he never had:

His advice to anyone—black or white—is that most young people in this day and age, especially in Britain, have great opportunities through education and should take full advantage of them. Don't act the big person and leave school thinking you'll get a job straight away and if you do, it won't be such a good one as the one you would have got if you had followed your education through.[9]

Pakistanis too have been relentless promoters of education through their own communities. Organised through a network of local mosques, and more recently through the Pakistan Muslim Centre, which has begun a literacy campaign among Pakistani men and women, the Pakistani community has been running its own Koranic schools and mother tongue classes for many years. It has also campaigned successfully to have Urdu taught in a number of secondary schools where there are concentrations of

Pakistani young people, and many school students have studied GCSE Urdu and achieved a high level of success.

A new belongingness

Many Pakistanis of the original arrivant generation thought that they would come to England to work 'just for five years', and then return to buy some land in Kashmir or build a better house for their family—and perhaps another too to rent out. But somewhere along the way a new feeling of belonging to England—and Sheffield—developed, that caused them to rethink and finally to decide to stay. To stay, to make a life for their families to build and struggle to carry on working, to contribute and to help make a lasting community in a particular neighbourhood in north-east Sheffield. Almost in despite of himself and his life of endless work an elderly Pakistani concludes:

> I came to Sheffield solely for the work. But perhaps this city has become my home. I remember the English people I've worked with in Sheffield. I cannot think of the possibility of living outside Sheffield. This is my home.[10]

Such deep feeling of being a part of a community—in spite of the pain and the struggle that there has been—is what makes its people want to claim it, make it survive and develop, make it worth living in. Yet such a decision, when your origins and connections are with another country, the country of your birth, your history or your culture is not an easy one. It often has to be made by children too, and takes some expenditure of thought and emotion:

> **My Two Countries**
> I was born in Britain
> In the town of Sheffield.
> Sheffield is the city, I learned everything I know,
> Sheffield is the city for me.
> Her cold air is, in me, no matter where I go,
> My mind, my heart won't leave the place,
> The place is so dear to me.
> I would love to go to Yemen
> The country of my ancestors
> To breathe the sweet warm air
> And taste the freshly-picked fruit.
> I am so proud to be a Yemeni
> I won't change that for the whole wide world!
> I want to be a part of building a better and brighter future
> for the whole world
> In which the peoples
> Great and small,

> Rich and poor,
> Black and white
> Live in a happy and healthy world!
> But deep, deep down inside,
> Sheffield is the place I long to stay.
>
> Nadia (1 4)

These are precious words indeed. For they show in a young person a new bonding, a commitment to a city that she now holds as her own. And such young people perhaps because they often show no fear of love, express this new belonging in these terms—as in the following poem, written by, Safa, a fourteen year old girl from the Yemen, who had been in Sheffield and learning English for only six months.

The future of Sheffield
This is the place I live in
The place I love.
Sheffield is my place
Sheffield is my country.
I came here and I don't know why -
Maybe because I want to stay here
Or because I love it, or... or... or...
I don't know, but the thing I do know is
That I don't want to leave it.

It's a nice place for all people
Its hands are always open for all people,
For every kind of people, every colour of people—
They're never closed, its hands, never ... never ...
We have to make it more beautiful.

I find no sentimentality in these poems, although it may be difficult for some to accept that communities who have suffered so much from racism, oppression and injustice through the years can talk of love for the place where all this has come to pass. But if a new community is to be forged within the smithy of our inner cities, it can be made only out of such strength of belonging and dedication. And the school must house it and nurture it, through its own commitment to its community and that community's youth. For the school has a commission to support and prepare its students to create, advance and serve that community—in the way in which a new generation of Yemenis took the responsibility from their parents to struggle for betterment after the shattering blow of mass redundancies in the early eighties, which threatened to demoralise and cripple the entire community. The tasks of leadership became theirs, it was up to them to struggle now for their parents' generation too:

The young Yemenis looked at all these problems and said, on behalf of the entire community, 'We can't continue like this! Our circumstances are bad, they require us to struggle. We need to use the time and energy we have now to organise ourselves as working class people who are unemployed and who need a better way of life.' It was the results of the conversations we had with our parents about such themes that caused us to build the community organisations that we still have now.[11]

Releasing ambition

Within the black working class communities there are strong educational ambitions and high expectations for their young people. Such aspirations have almost always characterised the arrivant consciousness, and this often contrasts markedly with the predetermined routes in life which white working class parents foresee for their children. In this sense too, black parents and their sons and daughters are helping to lift the horizons of inner city communities. They have left one country for another, with *education* as one of their most passionate objectives. They will not surrender it. Caribbean parents, for example, have seen children—although not necessarily their own, given the hard and expensive struggle that often exists in the islands to secure a full secondary education—succeed and achieve brilliantly in schools in Jamaica, Barbados and Trinidad. They, and parents from Pakistan, Yemen and Somalia are accustomed to being *ambitious* for their children and their communities and want to see that ambition released and fulfilled.

Thus they have often been justly frustrated and angered at an education system which sometimes seems to scoff at their ambition—or at teachers who have patronised them or quietly sniggered between themselves at them, or 'sensitively' disillusioned them when, in their faltering English or Caribbean dialect, they told them how they wanted their son or daughter to be a doctor, an architect or a lawyer. How many times have their children been directed towards more 'appropriate' non-academic courses and an early departure from the education system? The shame of this truth is that it often happened in the comprehensive schools that should have been there to satisfy their ambitions and respond enthusiastically to their high expectations, schools that were all that the community had.

For the school must be there, in the community, in order to *release* and *realise ambition* which is such a dynamic source of motivation for all children. And not just for their individual futures, but for the future of their community too—as in the plans of this thirteen year old Yemeni girl. It is not a selfish, bourgeois, exploitative ambition that she invokes. It is for her and of her as a part of her community. That is how she wishes to see her future:

My ambitions are to be a lawyer, or even a doctor. I would like to go straight into college when I leave school, get high A levels, study Law and get a degree at University.

I've wanted to be a lawyer since I was eleven years of age. I want to defend innocent people in the high courts of Justice.

Hopefully, when I've completed my education, I will be able to serve my own community as a person who can help people.

Partnership?

In the publicity material that comes out from local education authorities, much is written about the 'partnership' between schools and local communities. It is true that many schools are indispensable as the hubs of their local neighbourhoods, offering resources during daytimes and evenings and bringing a cohesion that no other institution can offer. This is why, when such schools are threatened with closure, there is often so much fierce resistance and campaigning. But in many other contexts this proclaimed partnership has been one of LEA rhetoric and wish-fulfilment, and to its constituents the school has remained a detached and forbidding centre with little real interest in offering its considerable space and resources to its surrounding working class community. Baker's 1988 Act takes full account and advantage of this common dissatisfaction, and instead of bolstering inner-city schools and working to help improve their performance, only seeks to reduce and dismember them and encourage their parents to send children to larger and richer schools in the middle-class suburbs. Thus formal 'catchment areas'—supplying local schools with local students—have been abolished and so-called 'parental choice' is being championed. So the Act is threatening to create a generation of long-distance students and faraway schools, and in the minds of working class parents helps to legitimise the fear of 'local' education in nearby comprehensive schools.

For these parents may ask, why should I send my child to a school which cannot guarantee academic success? Which has no wall-to-wall honours boards like the ex-grammar school an the other side of the city? That never talks about getting its pupils to Oxford or Cambridge? That, compared to the school in the high-price property suburbs has a poor record of academic success. Where children have been regularly seen scrapping outside the school gates or pushing and shoving at bus stops? Where there is no grammar school feeling or discipline?

These are key questions continually put, and should never be ignored, cold-shouldered or answered by empty rejoinders of egalitarian ideology or platitudes about the moral superiority of sending your child to the local school. For all these questions stem from a progressive understanding—that working class children, black and white, should have the best possible education and it is the responsibility of the parent to make sure that they secure it. The responsibility of the 'community school' must be to provide this, and along with the commitment to community must also come a commitment to excellence, excellence in the local—the development of excellence in the heart of the community itself Many working class comprehensive schools of the seventies and eighties built reputations of being very *caring* schools and heavy resources and investment were put into their pastoral systems—often at the direct expense of concentrating upon academic achievement. This created a problem of unbalance and sometimes a debasement of the original comprehensive school project of levelling opportunities upward for the children of the working class. There was also a liberal notion in currency amongst teachers that somehow education, in becoming more 'relevant' to the community, should also become less 'stressful' for working class children, with curriculum becoming lighter, less academic, less pressurised—that the school's emphasis should be upon caring and accommodation rather than stretching and aspiring for the working class child, whom, it was often asserted 'couldn't manage' the discipline and intensity of academic rigour.

Of course, this thinking was powerfully mistaken and led to much diluted curriculum, of unchallenging 'projects' and worksheets, of unguided individualism that was passed off as 'creativity', of confusion over language policy which led to a downgrading of Standard English (caricatured as a 'middle class' language and therefore irrelevant to white and black working class children). Routines of study often became slack—there was a fashion for seeing homework as 'counter productive' because it became more and more difficult to insist upon and collect, and habits of quiet, concentrated study or writing were seen as less important than the continuous 'interaction' of organised (and sometimes disorganised) groupwork. In short, in many contexts real progress was replaced by progressivism which was often more about teaching slogans and catchwords than real advancement for the student. Some teachers turned away from reading and print literacy, arguing that the 'media revolution' required first and foremost 'media literacy' and it became more common to use the video to impart information, than to read and imagine. With so much that was new coming into the curriculum, time management and concentration upon the reading-emphatic 'traditional' pedagogy became more and more difficult for teachers. Allocation of subject time and curriculum congestion meant that students often experienced a little of everything, but missed the essentials of foundation skills like reading, writing and mathematics, that were usually still the main curriculum force in the suburban comprehensives and ex-grammar schools. Basic literacy—punctuation, spelling, sentence structure—and numeracy began to suffer.

Thus the smaller, local, working class comprehensive schools became to be associated with the underachievement of white and black working class children at the same time that they began to refer to themselves as 'community schools'. Despite the fine work and achievement which many of them offered to their communities, they too began to suffer from a stereotype, which was sometimes partly of their own making. Thus many working class parents who saw education associated with aspiration and wanted their children to reach institutions of higher education, started to abandon and leapfrog their local comprehensive and sent their children further afield, where they considered the standards *must* be higher. Once such a view of the local school was locally established, it became very difficult to change, and sibling and peer pressure often made the boycott of local schools almost automatic by large sections of the communities. 'Community schools' then took on an inferior status, became associated with the stereotypes of low-attainment and black children, and pricked the sometimes latent racism within working class communities into noxious life. It was this overall scenario that Kenneth Baker exploited through his Education Act, prising open and inflaming the misconceptions and doing nothing to repair the weaknesses. His legislation proclaimed and appeared to give more 'choice' of schools to parents. But as many schools rapidly diminished in numbers, and LEAs, dutifully following the 'pupil number-driven' criteria of the Act (colluding with Baker by citing 'non-viability' in teaching the 'National Curriculum' as their reason) moved in to close the local comprehensives, working class parents in fact were left with no choice at all. The only expedient left to them was education out of the community since there was now no local school. It had already closed and the nearest school was now some distance away out of the neighbourhood. Thus 'parental choice' became nothing more than a phantom slogan, and a device by a conservative government for removing precious educational resources from struggling inner-city communities.

Survive and develop

The first task facing inner-city comprehensives at the present time is thus to *survive,* is not to be closed down by local education authorities zealously trying to economise and rationalise under pressure of government cuts to their aggregated schools budget. They must expect to fight closure plans and campaign for survival as a part of their way of life and mainstream curriculum. They will certainly not be given any peace or space in these last years of the century. But they can grasp and use *campaigning* in constructive ways, both as an integral part of a curriculum of community resistance and as a means of rallying support from the community and bringing together its disparate groups in cooperative involvement in the work of the campaign. In the process of the campaigning the School can also begin to re-profile and re-orientate itself, if necessary, towards excellence *and* community, so as to throw off any previous identification with the soft and diluted version of 'Community education' that may have damaged its credibility with local parents in the past.

'Community schools' always proclaimed the principle of 'involving' parents and community as a part of their liberal philosophy, but sometimes managed this 'involvement 'in paternalistic ways, telling the community how and when it should be involved and choosing the activities on its behalf. The school set the curriculum for the community, rather than the reverse. A different approach to community participation needs to be developed, so that community organisations use the school as their centre, that they feel that the buildings and resources are genuinely theirs to use, develop and protect. In this way the out-of-school-hours activities will link directly with, reinforce and heighten motivation for what happens in official school hours—whether they be mother tongue schools, supplementary classes, cultural events, religious gatherings, community meetings or sports initiatives.

Of course, developing a tradition of excellence is a long and hard struggle for a school, particularly an inner-city school which is underfunded, under-resourced, understaffed and continually living with a terminal threat from its own local education authority. And yet such schools have no choice but to discard their old stigmas of underachievement and respond positively to the genuine ambitions of working class parents for their children. There is no other way. But this does not mean meekly submitting to the strictures and deformity of the National Curriculum, testing and all the attendant paraphernalia of narrow and twisted knowledge. It means working closely with parents and families to find projects and alternatives which aim to develop and enrich their lives and communities. It also means reestablishing in the lives of school students basic habits and routines of study and work discipline, through contracts and an understanding of the particular responsibilities of school, parents and the students themselves. It means developing with the students democratic responsibilities so that they have and exert much more control over their own discipline and opportunities. And at the centre of development there must be brought forward strategies of *emulation*, using exemplars and models from the communities using the school—those young people who have already succeeded in a spectrum of pursuits and activities need to be persuaded to keep in continuous contact with the school, to be available to those students striving to succeed and to be motivators for those who are lacking enthusiasm and purpose. By visiting the school regularly and talking formally and informally to students, acting as mentors, counsellors and sources of emulation, they will help to stimulate ambition and continually lift up expectations

But more than anything else, the school which serves the community does, not simply receive and transmit knowledge from other sources or through "orders' like those from the Department of Education and Employment, setting out the content of the 'National Curriculum'. The school, working with the community it serves, makes knowledge, produces scholarship, creates participation and culture. It records its community's own story through a multilingual campaign of oral history; it struggles against high levels of heart disease amongst its community's old people by preventative health literacy work; it seeks to understand the basis of its community's economy and industrial resources by work experience and work research; it teaches, learns and proudly expresses all its languages and cultures; it studies the human geography of the world through its community's own internationalist experience and creates, performs and publishes its poetry, music and drama through what it learns; it forges its technology according to the community's needs that surround and press down upon it. The curriculum of the 'living school' lives with the realities of the close and distant world around it, and the soul of the people and their communities who use it, enrich it—and by enriching it, are developed through it.

Notes

1 This, and the quotations from the poems which follow, are from Searle, Chris, (Ed.): *Children of Steel: a Sheffield anthology*. Sheffield City Libraries, 1988.
2 Coard, Bernard, *How the West Indian child is made educationally sub normal in the British school system*, New Beacon Books, London 1970.
3 For this, and following quotations see Searle, Chris and Shaif, Abdulgalil, 'Drinking from one pot: Yemeni unity at home and overseas', *Race and Class* April-June 1991, Institute of Race Relations, London.
4 Majumdar, Pritish: *From Bangladesh to Attercliffe*: Sheffield Education Department, 1986.
5 Quoted in 'Wordmakers'', Searle, Chris: *All Our Words*, Young World Books, London, 1986.
6 Gure, Ibrahim: 'A refugee from Somalia', *Dialogue*, Summer 1991, Sheffield Education Department.
7 *Daily Mail*, 31, July 1991 and 3, August 1991
8 Iqbal, Ara and Van Riel (Compilers), *Just for Five Years:Reminiscences of Pakistani Senior Citizens in Sheffield*, Sheffield City Libraries, 1990
9 Hussain, Ghafoor, *Doing his Share: a study of a Pakistani worker by his son*, Earl Marshal School, Sheffield, 1991.
10 Iqbal, Ara and Van Riel op. cit.
11 Searle and Shaif op. cit.

CAMPAIGNING *IS* EDUCATION   (1993)

Education, particularly secondary education, in the inner cities in Britain is under attack and vulnerable. As the impact of Conservative legislation (from 1988 onwards) and the market system of schooling pressurises local education authorities (LEAs), the dangers to schools in inner-city neighbourhoods—and working-class black and white families' educational prospects—are becoming greater and greater. Prime minister John Major has himself identified inner-city education with 'bad schools' that are 'academically bankrupt' and has threatened to 'bring in the liquidators' to close them.[1]

These threats were given substance in the White Paper on education, published by the secretary of state for education, John Patten, in July 1992. Besides constructing a framework to enable more and more schools to 'opt out' of LEA control, and thus render LEAs effectively powerless and schools almost totally subject to unplanned market pressures, new plans were introduced to create 'hit squads' of retired headteachers and inspectors. Officially termed 'Educational Associations', these will have powers to intervene directly and take over inner-city schools, and as the *Daily Mail* of 29 July 1992 put it run them 'in the same way as receivers attempting to rescue an ailing firm'.

This state of permanent jeopardy and insecurity over the educational futures of working-class people was always a part of the Tory educational reform project. For, by creating the fear among parents that their local education must always be second rate, they are continually tempted to abandon schools in their own working-class neighbourhoods, either for those in the wealthier and leafier suburbs which are generally bigger, appear more successful and often have a grammarian past — or for the elitist city technology colleges funded in part by private business and industry. Thus, the market seeks to remove working-class children's education from their own communities, and put local comprehensive schools at risk of closure. For, as such schools grow smaller, the LEAs themselves move in, at government behest, to close them—claiming that they hold too many 'surplus places' and are, therefore, uneconomical. To this is added the 'curriculum' argument that they have too few resources to cover effectively the broad demands of the government's national curriculum. In this way, even erstwhile progressive LEAs follow the market and become the unwilling servants of the Conservative attack on working-class education.[2]

Yet these LEAs are elected, predominantly, by working-class people who entrust the well-being of local services including their schools to them. More and more, such LEAs are choosing not to stand up to or find creative solutions to central government legislation, but to succumb to it. Thus, inner-city secondary schools find themselves almost permanently vulnerable to the threat of closure. For them, campaigning is not an occasional expedient. It is a continuous process. Therefore, such schools must ask the question: how can we turn campaigning from a laborious, exhausting chore into an advantage? How can a campaigning process spark genuine educational progress? How can it mobilise community support and re-charge a curriculum of resistance? How can it give new life to schools condemned by both the Conservative government and Labour LEAs to the brink of existence?

For progressive governments elsewhere in the world which have attached a popular premium to education, the notion of the *campaign* in educational policy and practice has been paramount. Rather than it being forced upon them, it has been consciously chosen as central to their process and inextricably linked with the day-to-day organisation of education and the mobilisation of their peoples. Through making mainstream education a continuous campaign in itself, revolutionary processes such as those in Cuba, Nicaragua, Ethiopia or Grenada made substantial advances, reaching sections of the population hitherto untouched by effective educational provision.[3] These campaigns have set particular targets around adult and child literacy, success in study or examinations, university entry and the training of teachers, and have been the vehicles for genuine progress in all these areas. Once again, those struggling for educational development, or the rejected in the inner cities of Europe and North America, could learn much from the campaigning energy and genius of the organisers and programme managers of processes in the progressive governments and liberation movements of the Third World. What follows is an account of how one, small, local inner-city school, forced into fighting for its survival, was strengthened both in educational terms and in terms of its community links.

Divide and school

In February 1991, Sheffield's education department published its 'schools review', with one of its major objectives 'removing surplus places by rationalisation and closure of schools'. This was linked to issues of small schools and their 'viability' or otherwise to manage the newly introduced national curriculum. One of the schools named for possible closure under these criteria was Earl Marshal Comprehensive School in north-east Sheffield, an inner-city school with a gradually increasing roll of 420 students from local white, Yemeni, Pakistani, Somali and Caribbean families. It was offered as an 'alternative closure' to that of Herries School, another comprehensive some two miles away from Earl Marshal, serving an all-white council estate. The reasons for closure were summarised thus:

> Earl Marshal is a small school. It has many surplus places and will be severely constrained financially under Local Financial Management; with

significant consequences for its ability to deliver the National Curriculum.
Closure would assist the financial viability of neighbouring schools.[4]

In addition, the 'very poor' state of the roof of one of the school's buildings was
apparently another decisive factor.

These 'reasons' for closing a thriving school in a working-class neighbourhood,
strongly supported by the local communities and parents, seemed dubious to many.
They appeared to have no educational foundation, making pupil numbers, LEA
budgetary factors and an unpopular national curriculum the prime determinants. In
addition, the LEA appeared to be openly setting school against school, putting a
predominantly 'white' school and a predominantly 'black' school against each other
in a fight for survival, and also declaring that the closure of one would benefit those
schools that remained open, thereby seeking to gain the support of those that would
survive against those condemned to closure. If the government had wanted to write a
more blatant 'divide and rule' script for a local education authority, it could not have
done better than this, which the LEA had written for itself.

This divisiveness was rejected by the headteachers of Earl Marshal and Herries in a
joint declaration on the very day the schools review was announced. They publicly
pledged to work together in a unified campaign aimed at saving both schools and
ensuring them a secure and successful future. The other schools plus the tertiary college
in the northern 'cluster' of the city, after a number of meetings and discussions, also
came together and issued a 'declaration'. This made a number of points against the
closure of either school including that 'all of the Cluster institutions believe that there
is quality education from nursery to tertiary college, available for the people in this
part of Sheffield.' Full access to this provision should be allowed to continue to develop.'
Out of the threat of dismemberment had come a new unity.

In order to survive, the school had to campaign. It was, in fact, the best thing that
could have happened to the school and its people, to its students, teachers, parents and
communities. It took all concerned into the strongest and most conscious form of
education, and created a new cohesiveness that would be a must for its development
after survival. We had a short-term objective, of resisting and avoiding closure; but
within it. also, a long-term aim, to bring together all the elements of school life and
mobilise them to transform the working of the school so that the threat of closure—
ever prevalent for a small inner-city school like ours—would never be carried through.

There were several dimensions to Earl Marshal's campaign strategy. The major one
was to create an involvement of all those who used the school in the struggle for its
survival. Teachers met to consider ways of ensuring that the theme of resistance to
closure went through all their curriculum areas. This meant badge-making, banner-
making and poster design in the science, art and technology departments, a competition
of protest songs in the music department, and a surge of poetry, essays and letter-

writing in English lessons. The languages department ensured that a multilingual aspect was given to the campaign through the organisation of an international community concert on the theme of resistance to closure, and banners were made of slogans in Arabic, Urdu and Somali, as well as English. Strip posters in banner headlines were also produced on school computers.

All this helped to create a culture of protest throughout the school and the adjacent youth centre, which was used by the students during their lunch break. This spread quickly to other school users and workers as the Somali, Yemeni and Pakistani communities met to discuss their contributions to the campaign, and one of the cleaners coordinated the organisation of a neighbourhood petition in support of both the threatened schools. The local tertiary college organised a public meeting with the same objective, and 300 local people attended, expressing in moving words and speeches their loyalty to the schools and the work they did. People reaffirmed their wish and right to have secondary schooling close at hand, both to educate their children and remain a centre of community life and development. Councillors and education officers were invited to listen to the full force of a working-class community's regard and attachment to its schools that night, and were left in no doubt as to how much it valued and depended on local education. 'Our second home', was how a Pakistani governor described Earl Marshal, and a local grandmother wept as she told the councillors how her grandchildren would have to break strong friendships they had made with other students and teachers at Herries, and be forced to travel across the city to school, if Herries were closed: 'Why should our children have to do this?' she asked. 'Why is it always our children?' As others pointed out that, in the more prosperous parts of the city, large secondary schools untouched by the review sat side by side, her question had a sharp pertinence.

The communities uniting

Although the students' friendships regularly crossed over the lines of culture, race and language, the same was not true in their parents' experience. But the campaign to save the school developed gradually into an effective catalyst to bring the parent communities together in the struggle against closure. At the beginning of the campaign, the Yemenis and Pakistanis were working separately. They had their own support meetings at their own centres. By the end of the process, they were meeting together to plan the demonstration outside the school that greeted the leader of the council when he came to visit. Even within their own community structures, the campaign served to consolidate cohesion. When the Yemenis organised their own picket of the school during a consultation visit by the education officer in charge of the review, the gathering created a little moment of history within their own ranks, as well as pointing to future efforts at unity. As Abdulgalil Shaif, speaking on behalf of the Yemenis, told the Sheffield *Star:*

It is the first time men and women have picketed together like this and it shows the strength of feeling within the community... They see this as just the start of the fight. If the school closes they will lose twenty years of struggle to get the facilities they have today. We would also like to hold another protest— perhaps with other black groups in the city.'[5]

Local Pakistani parents also overcame internal tensions in order to fight for the school's future. Previous rivalries between mosque leaders were put aside as Pakistani parents attended a support meeting in school, called and organised by themselves. Representatives from three different mosques affirmed how important the school was to them as a community centre—and as if to underline the point, as one of them spoke, the large class of Koranic and Urdu students arrived at the school and walked through the meeting in order to reach their afterschool lesson. The meeting reminded the officer present from the LEA that these classes are run on a nightly basis—just as the Yemenis had stressed how 170 young people from their community use the school for three hours every Saturday and Sunday for their Arabic language school. For the Pakistanis, the campaign appeared to signal a strong commitment to local state education. There was no talk of separate Islamic schools, which had been on the agenda a few years before. As Rashid Ahmad of the local Pakistani Social and Cultural Society explained: 'We are looking for progressive and broad education—we are not going backwards. We will promote a close relationship with other communities and we have been delighted with the cooperation so far.'[6] The irony was that, five years previously, the LEA had criticised Islamic communities for calling for separate schools; now they were threatening to close down the very local school where they had encouraged Asian parents to send their children, and those same parents were defending it vigorously! Abdulgalil Shaif expressed this rejection of separatism unequivocally to Fiona Walters, the Sheffield *Star* journalist: 'The Yemeni community finds it a nonsense to think of separate schools', for they already had their own supplementary school within the very buildings that the LEA were threatening to close.

This new unity across the communities in support of the school was also emphasised by Afro-Caribbean parent governor Lambert Poyser, who, in the same *Star* article, told of his house-to-house work:

Because of the Review, I have knocked on doors and talked to a lot of people about education—something I would not normally do ... Everyone has been cooperative and Afro-Caribbean families are being drawn back to Earl Marshal. A few years ago it seemed to me that they weren't interested in Earl Marshal, but now they see what is happening there and they are attracted back ... I hope now that parents remain united and that they get even more united.

These communities all sent strong and supportive letters to the education department and the leader of the council. The first, sent very early in the campaign by the Somali Community Association, caused a considerable rethink in the education offices, as did a powerful message from the Sheffield and District Afro-Caribbean Community Association, which 'expected the council to protect and safeguard the educational aspirations of our children and their families', emphasising that the closure of the school would be 'a massive step backwards.' The local white community, too, pitched in. The Grimesthorpe Residents Association, which held a public meeting in support of the school, put strong stress on how they valued the multiracial chemistry of the school, while also showing the very real dangers facing children having to go further afield for their everyday education:

> Children have been naturally integrated from the nursery school and grow together, not noticing the skin's colour but knowing one another as friends. This could be lost by moving these children to different areas where they may find it difficult to integrate freely because basic friendships from infancy are not there.
>
> We do not believe that any school should close; maybe your books will look better but children are far more important than book-keeping. So think about the tiny tots who, if Earl Marshal closes, will have to travel way out of their district to a school across the dreaded Firvale Roads where many accidents have happened ... Older people are scared of crossing these roads, so heaven help the young ones. By closing either Earl Marshal or Herries you will be forcing children from these communities on to these dangerous roads to get to the school of *your* choice not theirs.

These arguments were concrete, local and reflected the extra strain and division put upon working-class people if their local school were lost to them. They showed such a community taking account of itself, defending what it had, resisting arbitrary and ignorant decisionmaking that would have a profound and damaging effect upon its daily lives and routines. The campaign was becoming a crucible for local people, making them stronger and more cohesive, while also instructing the councillors and officers who made decisions in their names to come out of their offices and cabals and work with them. Abdulgalil Shaif put this very succinctly to the *Star*.

> Before the Review came out there was very little contact between the different communities. But the school is a life-line, it is the heart of the whole area. Now, as a result of the campaign to keep it open, other issues have come forward which communities can tackle together. For example, we have built a Yemeni and Pakistani group which will took at common issues which affect us both and we have also closer links with the Somali, Caribbean and white communities. It is very important that these links continue and that

local politicians seize the opportunity to try and work in partnership with the people.

Campaign and curriculum

Throughout Earl Marshal School, the campaign became the single most important curriculum issue. Students, like their parents, began to take stock of the usefulness of the school to them. They wrote essays in their English lessons, which many changed into letters which were then sent to councillors and the chief education officer. These were not generally sloganising or emotional, but contained strong arguments for the retention of the school. One 13-year-old white girl wrote:

Earl Marshal should not be closed down as:
(a) Children would have to go to schools far away from their homes.
(b) By going to Earl Marshal we will easily be able to go to college and universlty, which we are nearly all intending to do.
(c) We would lose contact with all our friends.
(d) There is no other school with a youth club that can be used at dinner time and at night.
(e) There is no other school where we can learn Arabic in our own time.

And a fifth-year Yemeni girl added her reasons, pointing out that she had come from the Yemen only a year before—and this was the level of her English:

I think the school should not be closed for a lot of reasons, like:
1   Earl Marshal is a centre which is involved in the Arabic and Urdu schools and communities.
2   It is the nearest school to the area in which the children live, so they should not need to catch a bus on their own to go to school.
3   It has the adult education where women who did not have their chance to go to school went there because it is near to their homes.
4   It has a sports centre in which we do PE in the school, a youth club, good facilities and good education.
5   It is near to the nursery in which we could take our brothers and sisters without being late.

The rhetoric, rhyming, slogans and emotion were expressed in the poems and song lyrics written throughout the campaign. Some of the rhymes made themselves and expressed pride and exuberance:

Asians, Somalis, Saudis, Syrians, English and Yemenis
We all come to this school, and we're not enemies!

Other poems were performed at assemblies and community events, and seemed to be expressing what most people, students and parents, genuinely felt:

Why should our school be closed down?
I don't want to go to another school at the other end of
town.
I like Earl Marshal School because the teachers are kind,
So come on, don't be blind
The people of our community need this school, I think
you'll find.
You say you'll shut our school in 1992
But who are you?
We have many cultures in our school—
Somalis, Pakistanis, Asians and Yemenis.
Not only do children use this school
Adults and parents use it too.
We have a Youth Centre and a Sports Centre too.
Without these things what would the locals do?
So put these thoughts into consideration,
Just stop and think before you ruin our education!
Matthew (14)

or:

To close Earl Marshal you've got to be a fool,
Because Earl Marshal is a great school!
I'm in full-time education at Earl Marshal
And I want it to stay that way,
And none of you can push me away!
I know all the teachers
And all the features.
To close this school down you've got to be a fool!
You think packing a school in
Is as easy as throwing rubbish in a bin.
Well, you're wrong!
I've been at Earl Marshal for over a year,
And I'm not moving, I'm staying right here!
To close a school for good
You'd need to padlock the door.
But if you do you'll be asking for a war!
We'll take a vote to rule you out,
I know we'll win without a doubt.
The school has great fame and a name,
To close it down would be a shame.
The school won't close.
We're going to fight for it,

        every inch, every step,
        Every little bit!

                                                Faheem (I 4)

And Nadia, a 14-year-old Yemeni, student. brought the struggle together in the brief,
clear lines of her poem which was read out over the local radio:

        We'll do more than fight
        To get our equal rights.
        If you're asking for a fight
        You'd better think twice!
        Our school teaches us,
        We don't make no fuss,
        We've got trust in our teachers
        And they've got trust in us.
        So listen here Council.
        Please don't close our school,
        Please do not be cruel -
        It's because we love this school.

The poetry was not confined to students. Margaret Barraclough, a 67-year-old local
poet, ex-steel worker, fork-lift driver and now a member of the Chuffinelles satirical
group, visited the school, read her poetry and taught a session to some of the students.
She was very moved by their creative response and sent back to the school these verses
of her own, dedicated to its struggle:

        When I first made a visit here
        And met you and some of your tutors,
        For the first time in years I began to think That there was
        some hope for the future.

        And these school-closing maniacs, you could teach them
        something too,
        Maybe you could help them see the light.
        'Cos I'm sure if they spent a few hours with you
        They might get their priorities right.

The campaign climaxes

All through the weeks and months of the campaign an enormous effort had been put
into sending into the LEA counter-figures, counterstatistics and counter-documentation
which refuted, replaced and disproved the figures, miscalculations and information
contained in the schools review. The school had to scrutinise itself very closely and
find proof of all it attested in its rejoinders to the council. Thus, it began to know itself

more closely than ever—from the minutiae of budget, details of student number predictions, local birthrate, neighbourhood housing situation, the truths that the district it served has the worst unemployment rate, worst post-16 staying-on rate, worst petty crime rate, worst heart disease fatality rate in the city. And yet they were proposing to close its only secondary school! The blitzkrieg on the LEA included letters and representations from local employers and industrialists, social workers and career officers, academics who had done research in the school, ex-students, ex-teachers, local MPs like David Blunkett and Richard Caborn—as well as from students, parents and local community organisations.

In the final week before the LEA announced its interim changes to the review, we invited councillor Clive Betts, the leader of the council, and one of his senior colleagues in charge of the council budget to visit the school and hear representations from students and parents. They were received outside the school by a large demonstration. While inside the school the students continued to work at their lessons, their parents, carrying banners in the languages of the school and of their own communities—Somali, Urdu, Arabic and English—which had been made in the technology department, expressed the hope that 'Earl Marshal school would live forever!' Student representatives from every class lined up to present letters typed up on the school's wordprocessors, expressing the collective wishes of their classmates. As Councillor Betts walked upstairs to my office, carrying an armful of envelopes, and among a squad of student and parent representatives, the music teacher introduced the winning protest songs, which sang out through a large, deeply-bassed cassette recorder. The words were echoing in his ears as he sat down, surrounded by the determined and persuasive community, and sipped a coffee:

> Don't hold back before it's too late -
> We want to be near our friends and mates.
> If our school closes, we'll have to go
> To different schools—where? Nobody knows.
> We've got different races here,
> We don't want them to disappear...

The next ninety minutes brought all elements of the school together to discourse with Councillor Betts: teachers, students, governors, Yemenis, Pakistanis, Afro-Caribbeans, Somalis, the Grimesthorpe residents and school management. There was no invective, no harangues; only reasoned argument, convincing example and clear principle, as speaker after speaker made their contribution. The school was speaking, with many voices and from a cosmopolitan spectrum of experience, but with one common commitment: it should be allowed to survive, grow and develop. As the councillors listened and responded with carefully chosen and cautious words, I thought of the words in one of the leader's envelopes, written by a 15-year-old Yemeni girl who had been in England only half a year: 'Really this school is like a heart. Just think if you close a big heart down, what will happen ... think.'

Why campaign?

When we heard, less than a week later, that, alongside Herries School, our school was to be removed from the closure list in the schools review, our first reaction was to change the theme of our forthcoming community concert: from 'Save our School!' to a celebration. Now it was an opportunity to thank all those who had supported and worked for us. But more than that: we knew we had been right. We had refused to be divided from other schools named for closure that could have been seen as our 'rivals'. We had campaigned together, grouping with other schools where there were black and working-class communities in order to find strength and common ground.

For what is a successful campaign, if not an education and an exercise in popular, active democracy? Our school had been saved by ordinary working-class people of three generations, mobilising themselves, organising themselves, producing through their own creative energy the power, rationale and intellectual fire to think, speak and act for their own and their children's future. Here was a relatively obscure, small neighbourhood school with no great academic or grammarian tradition and the most unmilitant of names, in the heart of the most struggling section of a large British ex-industrial city, many of whose citizens were unemployed, from scattered parts of the decolonised world, standing up and actively taking part in something dear to their culture and future. The campaign had brought about that participation, that very activity that would create further development. And as the school was determined to carry on with its developmental work too, in the midst of its campaigning, it made development and survival synonymous. As it opened its new cricket centre, affirming the sporting enthusiasm and culture of, in particular, its Caribbean and Pakistani communities, it had used the occasion to proclaim its campaign. Devon Malcolm, the Jamaican-born, locally-bred international cricketer, in opening the centre named after him, spoke strongly against the closure and for the strength of community, just as Imran Khan, one of the greatest cricketers ever, and captain of Pakistan, had done some weeks earlier. As it publicised its 'Contracts of Study', striving to improve and make more routinised habits of serious study among its students, it did so in the context of the campaign. During the intervals of the school play, speeches in support of the school were made. When the protest songs were judged, the adjudication was made by Clive Rowe, a singer then performing a major role in the West End production of *Carmen Jones*. He too spoke up for the school to the local press. The school became saturated with the spirit of protest and cultural resistance to the closure, and its future development was bound to be marked by it.

But, for the parents, the campaign meant mobilisation for their Arabic language school, the continuation of their Urdu and Koranic classes and the upholding of their languages, religion and love of sport. It meant a further coming forward of their women, both mothers and daughters, a stubborn demonstration of community pride and culture and the continuation of hope in education to bring them progress—all an expression of the *popular* curriculum as opposed to the national curriculum. All this is why the campaign, once started, must go on and the school's function must be to carry it forward beyond survival to growth and community power — a different kind of achievement. As Marie, a 14-year-old student, aptly put it in a poem on the day after this little victory, and as it was read out by her Pakistani classmate at the celebration concert:

> Today's the day
> Our good news reigns.
> You people here
> Have taken pains
> To save our school,
> And see it shine.
> 'Can't stop us now
> We're in our prime!'

* * * * *

Yet, even as I revise this article for publication, the dangers to inner city schools like Earl Marshal and Herries grow more menacing. In an article headlined 'Bullish Patten intends to "mix it" with LEAs', the *Times Educational Supplement* reports on the new resolve of the secretary of state for education 'to crack down on council spending and surplus school places'.[7] The proposed new central government funding agencies for schools will be the prime vehicles of the crackdown, moving into areas where there are surplus school places' (particularly London, Birmingham, Sheffield and Manchester). In addition, the watchdogs of the national curriculum, the inspectors of the newly formed Office for Standards in Education (OFSTED), lambasted inner-city schools for 'failing' their students[8] in the same week (in October, 1993) that it was widely reported that, in the words of the *Observer's* education correspondent, 'the Government is to strip millions of pounds from schools in deprived inner-city areas'.[9] London LEAs are to be cut by up to £120m, and Birmingham and Bradford are also to suffer heavy losses. 'Local authorities with a large proportion of single-parent families and substantial ethnic minority populations will be the main losers.' continued the *Observer,* adding that 'affluent shire countries will gain the most'. The Government has thus made its intentions clear, and inner-city schools must continue to be on their campaigning guard.

Notes

1 *Guardian,* London, 17 June 1992.
2 See Searle, Chris, 'From Forster to Baker: the new Victorianism in education', *Race & Class,* April 1989.

3   See works like Hirson, S. and Butler, *J., And also teach them to read,* New York, 1983 or
    Lankshear, C. and Lawler, S., *Literacy, Schooling and Revolution,* Sussex, 1987; on Nicaragua,
    Kozol, Jonathan, *Children of the Revolution: a Yankee teacher in the Cuban schools,* New
    York, 1978; Searle, Chris, *Words Unchained: language and revolution in Grenada,* London,
    1984, and *A Blindfold Removed: Ethiopia's struggle for literacy,* London, 1990 and Bhola,
    H.S., *Campaigning for Literacy* , International Council for Adult Education, 1981, is an
    excellent description of literacy campaigning in a number of contexts throughout the world.

4   *Schools Review* , City of Sheffield Education Department, February 1991.

5   *Star* , Sheffield, 11 April 1991.

6   This and other quotations following from article by Fiona Walters in *Star* , Sheffield, 16 May
    1991.

7   *Times Educational Supplement* , 15 October 1993.

8   *Access and Achievements in Urban Education* , London, HMSO, 1993.

9   *Observer* , London, 31 October 1993.

PROUD TO SPEAK: LANGUAGES, RACISM AND UNITY (1992)

I want to begin by recalling an incident involving an encounter with some of our school's Yemeni students and a group of local young white men, on a Sheffield bus. Starting from the street and starting from language, it ends by unfolding a parable exposing much about the nature of racism in British society, and the habits and inclinations of those whose responsibility is supposed to be to protect us from it:

My friend, my aunt, my nephew and I got on the 93 bus going to Meadowhall. My aunt sat on the front seat of the bus and the rest of us sat at the back.

A man was sitting two seats behind my aunt and another man was sitting across from her with his girlfriend. My aunt started talking in Arabic. The man across from her told her to shut up. She asked 'why?'. He said, 'it is a gypsy language'. She said, 'I have nothing against you speaking the way you do'. He butted in and said: 'In England you speak English and in Iraq you speak Iraqi!'

I asked my aunt if everything was okay —and the same man said, 'shut up, you black bastard!'

My aunt went up to the bus driver and said 'have you heard the way he is talking?' The bus driver told the man to keep it down. And he answered, 'sorry English bus, English driver, I keep quiet'. Then my aunt asked him if he was racist. He said, 'No'; then he apologised. When my aunt got off the bus he said, 'Goodbye, sweetheart!'

He then asked my sixteen year old nephew to go over to him and shake his hand. He went over and my friend and I followed him. I sat behind my nephew and he sat across from the man, with my friend sitting behind him. Then the man said to my nephew: 'Who did you support in the war, England or Iraq?' My nephew said, 'None.' The man asked him again and I said, 'He doesn't believe in war.'

He got hold of my neck and said, 'I'm not talking to you!' Then my nephew moved the man's hands and the man head-butted him. My nephew started wrestling with him, and the man behind me hit my friend (cutting the top of his eye badly). Then I jumped on the man who hit my friend, and put him on the floor. I told my nephew and friend to run off the bus. So we ran away and went to the closest house we could find. The man who lived there got us a damp cloth for my friend's eye and called us a taxi so we would go to the police station where we thought we'd be safe.

While we were parked in the taxi, a silver car parked next to us and one of the people inside it said: 'That's the black bastards, let's kill them!' But the taxi driver drove off.

They still chased us all the way to the police station. At one point we stopped at the traffic lights and they got out of their car after they'd stopped too but we drove off and got to the police station at Attercliffe.

When we got in there they followed us in but the police came out and got them.

They said that they just wanted to talk to us.

The police put us all in different cells, then took our statements and let us go on bail.

Thus an incident which begins with racist insults regarding language against a group of young black British school students, ends with those who have been insulted being arrested, put in police cells, only finally to be released on bail by the police, and after they had voluntarily run into the police station for sanctuary from their racist attackers. In the whole context of the way in which the police treat young black people, it is not so unusual, and recalls the tragic events of January 1978 in Stoke Newington Police Station, in East London when the Caribbean youth, Michael Ferreira, was killed. Ferreira had been stabbed in Stoke Newington High Street by a gang of young whites, after they had insulted him and his friends with violently racist language. His friends, finding all the nearby telephone kiosks smashed, had carried the wounded Michael into the police station for help, and to make a telephone call for an ambulance. Despite Michael's condition, the police had harassed and accused them, delaying the crucial call while Michael's condition worsened. Ferreira died later of his wound, on an ambulance on the way to hospital.[1]

But here, in the Sheffield incident, in the beginning was language: fear of words and their meanings which you don't understand. Ironically, the attack took place outside the shining new stadium which was the venue for the 1991 World Student Games, a proclaimed internationalist extravaganza, constructed on the derelict site of Sheffield's massive but devastated steel industry, where the Yemeni immigrants (the fathers and grandfathers of these students) first worked as unskilled and low-waged workers at the bottom of the labour hierarchy, when they arrived from Aden and its hinterland in the fifties and sixties.[2] Yet still their language was the butt of insult and attack.

There is, of course, a further context of time: the aftermath of the 1991 Gulf War when anti-Arab racism reached a grim zenith in Britain, when every Muslim became an Iraqi and when every Arabic-speaker, Punjabi-speaker or black non-English speaker became a supporter and expatriate foot soldier of Saddam Hussein. These same Yemeni young people had a few weeks before, been stoned in their minibus as it made its way to Arabic language lessons in their community evening classes at a local school—their secondary school. Then the opening insult of the men on the bus and the reference to the 'Gypsy language', reflects a much older hatred: the centuries-old British racism against Romany and other travelling people. And this particularly is a part of Sheffield where signs in the windows and on the doors of local pubs give common notice that gypsies will not be served, and where only a few years ago a leader of the City Council had publicly proclaimed that all gypsies and their families should be clinically removed from Sheffield and its environs. Now the Yemenis found themselves pulled into this savage historical and cultural context by force of language, and ended up, like many a travelling person in history and now times, inside a police station cell.

So there need be nothing merely academic or metaphysical in talking or reflecting about language, culture and racism: those boys' experiences on the streets of Sheffield's East End could not have been more visceral and painfully felt. Such experiences are common to the lives of black young inner-city people, and they do not hold on to their language and assert its pride, dignity, love and usefulness without some courage and stamina. On other occasions this refusal to let go wins through in the end, as one Pakistani boy wrote in his Sheffield classroom:

> One day an incident happened to me when I was walking down the road, speaking to a friend in Punjabi.
>
> Some white boys came round the corner and made a circle around me. They started to ask me questions. They asked me,
>
> 'What's your name!'
>
> I said, 'Mohammed Islam.'
>
> They said, 'Are you a Paki?'
>
> I said, 'No, I am a Pakistani.'
>
> They said, 'Why are you in our country?'
>
> 'It's not your country', I said, 'God rules the universe, everything in the universe'.
>
> And they said, 'Don't speak your Paki language here. Go back to Paki-land and speak it there!'
>
> And I ran off home. I felt very insulted, but I bottled it up inside myself and told no-one.
>
> I stopped going down that road for a while. And later, when I did go back down there with my brother, they never said nothing.

The truth is that our bilingual school students often endure and resist agonising mental and physical batterings because of their first language. School often hands out such treatment in classroom, corridor and playground, and their languages are rendered invisible within its white and English-language culture—a culture fully buttressed and underlined by those who have designed and promoted the so-called National Curriculum across British state schools. They too, are telling our black children, in their moderated and hollow pedagogic tones, that they mustn't speak their gypsy language or their Paki-language here, that there is culture within the British school syatem that gives no place for such words of identity, certainly no *programmed*, curriculum place, and certainly no place for credit, recognition or achievement. They are, of course, as equally bad for all our young people as those who attack them on buses or in the street, or lock them in police cells when they speak the language which is theirs.

Constraining the Words

The aggression demonstrated in British culture against any other language but English runs throughout the organs and infrastructures of the life of the nation. This is bad enough if you are white and foreign, but if you are black and come from other national origins than Britain, there will be an additional racist dimension to this cultural hostility. This is felt particularly in many of our schools by black students, but when black adult readers open up the tabloid pages of the huge-selling daily newspapers like the *Sun* or the *Star* the expression of racist insults against their culture and languages is often intense. This tabloid curriculum is the vehicle for working class adults of the same narrowness, racism and national chauvinism so expressive in the 'National Curriculum' prescribed by British Tory educators which is offered to their children through the school system, and policed by OFSTED.

The tabloid curriculum has no time for the non-English languages of British black people. The *Sun* carries the flag high in making these attitudes clear on a daily basis. It regularly publishes stories about the indignation of individual white parents who discover that their children have learned Punjabi or Hindi words at school—even when the majority of a school's students speak these languages as their mother tongues. 'Less Punjabi here!' proclaimed a banner headline from the *Sun* in May 1987, telling the story of a white mother's anger when she discovered that her six year old son had learned at school to count from one to ten in that language—and he could recite Hickory, Dickory, Dock in Punjabi too![3] The implication in this article, and many similar stories in the *Sun*, is that the presence in British classrooms of black children and their own languages, is bound to be bad for white British children, polluting their culture, corrupting their language and bringing down educational standards. Another negative association—crime—was mixed into the concoction when the language of Benjamin Zephaniah, the rastafarian poet, was lampooned and his past was allegedly tied in with criminal activity: 'I am de crook, who stole de cash to print the book,'[4] mimicked the *Sun*'s leader writer in a grotesque imitation of a Creole dialect (reflecting the mocking answer of the Sheffield racist to the bus driver in the testimony that began this account).

Similarly, the new 'National Curriculum' gives no credence to Britain's other languages. The real' languages, the 'modern' languages are European languages. They form the languages of the new curriculum.' They are the legitimised tongues, the others spoken by black people, do not count—not Bengali, not Urdu or Punjabi, not Hindi, Chinese or Turkish, not Arabic, despite the hundreds of millions of human beings that speak these languages all over the world, as well as in Britain.[5] Recently, when in response to the growing number of Somali students who are entering our school, we looked for a GCSE syllabus so that they could study Somali and gain credit for their knowledge of the language, we discovered there was no such syllabus in any of the examination board lists. As far as recognition at the basic external examination level for the language of one of Britain's oldest black communities, their words and culture were invisible, non-existent.

As the 1988 Education Act and local management of schools bites deeper into the lives and finances of inner city schools and the scale of their budgets diminish, there is less money to pay teachers and less opportunity to staff Languages departments beyond what is often a very restricted number of teachers. This makes it difficult for schools to appoint teachers for languages other than those approved by the 'National Curriculum' regulations, even though they now formally have the power to appoint for whatever subjects they will. The teachers funded through the Home Office and 'Section 11' of the Local Government Act are required to teach English to the children of Commonwealth origins (and Pakistan). They cannot be recruited to teach the first languages of black children, and recent increased monitoring by the Home Office has made it more difficult to turn these resources for the teaching of Urdu, Bengali or other such languages, despite flexible teaching practices or a pedagogy that puts fluency and confidence in the first language as a requisite to be ready to master the second. And for the children of non-commonwealth countries like the Yemen, for example, 'Section 11' financed teachers could never legitimately be used—even to teach English in their first language, Arabic—as their country of origin disqualifies them from Home Office support. For the Home Office, as well as the Department of Education and Science, Arabic too is an invisible and silent language — a huge, racist vacuum in the life of British inner cities.

Resistance through language

So how does a school and its students, parents and teachers, many of whom speak, value, wish to learn and are determined to see taught the many languages that surround and express their lives, cultures and aspirations in the urban neighbourhoods where they live, study and work—how do they break free of such a mountain of constraints and barriers to their languages? What strategies and resources can they employ to assure a future for their tongues? How can they resist this uniformity of language being pressed upon them at school through the words which are theirs, for

> Your lips and tongue are also free, so let them be!
> Speak your feelings
> express how you feel... expressions of the morning dew,
> the stars and the moon
> which scrape the everlasting sky

       words can express
       what your mind intends to say
                                                    Nadia (14)

   And how can progressive state schools too, turn around this ignoring of their black
students' most powerful educational asset—their strength of language. Schools now
have control over their own budgets. They do not simply and meekly have to 'receive'
teachers from the local education authority. They are suddenly arbiters over whom
they recruit and select, despite the stranglehold of constraint imposed upon them by
central government, instructing them by their National Curriculum 'orders' what they
must or must not teach, or when and how they must 'test'. Yet for the first time inner
city schools theoretically have the space and control to choose independently who
their teachers will be, and what subjects they will teach. This is one rare benefit coming
from the Baker legislation. In our school this year, for the first time ever in Sheffield—
and as far as we know nationally—we appointed and are paying for from our own
budget, a permanent teacher of Arabic. Such choices are stark and need very careful
consideration, because an Arabic teacher comes as an alternative to another English,
Mathematics or Science teacher. The appointment is in no sense an 'extra', and small
inner city schools like ours have little enough flexibility within their staffing or their
timetabling. But we considered that an Arabic teacher was a priority for our Yemeni
and other Arabic-speaking students and felt that the small amount of Urdu teaching
offered by our bilingual English as a Second Language teachers predominantly to our
Pakistani students, needed to be matched by the teaching of Arabic. We are now
considering creative ways of ensuring the appointment of a Somali teacher, so that we
shall soon be able to offer that language at GCSE level to our Somali students, alongside
Urdu and Arabic, French and German. In this way we aim to keep faith with our black
communities who give so much to our school—by keeping faith with their languages
and securing the teaching of them, with the richness of their literatures, within the
open curriculum.
   The establishing and encouragement of community language schools attached to
inner-city state schools is a vital part of unleashing the full energy of the languages of
all communities being served by the school. These community language initiatives,
run at weekend or after-school sessions, have been pioneered by the organizations of
the communities, and have been tenaciously administered, and often continued through
difficult times of lack of accommodation, lack of finance, periods of heightened racism
(such as during the Gulf War) and shortage of qualified or trained teachers. Yet they
have always carried on, often growing from strength to strength. In Sheffield, for
example, a 1989 survey showed that 31 such language schools were operating in
community venues throughout the city in ten languages, with over 1500 learners taught
by 90 tutors.[6] Such educational activity and language learning has been generally

unacknowledged by and remained unconnected to the mainstream school system. This needs to change. Local state schools need to support these learning ventures which have been so crucial to community consolidation and development. They can offer classroom accommodation and resources like computers and libraries. They can help to train their volunteer teachers. They can bring in representatives from these classes onto their governing bodies, invite teachers from them into mainstream daytime classes and seek to make further connections through joint curriculum work, exchanges of teachers, school displays and community cultural events like concerts, publications and celebrations. Ways of accrediting the work done in the community classes also need to be developed, and recognition of their students' work documented in their school records of achievement. In our school, for example, both the local Pakistani mosque and the Yemeni Community Association use the classrooms for community-run Urdu and Arabic classes. The former meet every evening after school (plus Saturday mornings) and the Yemenis regularly have 170 students to their 3 hour Saturday and Sunday sessions.

Through our close relationships, we can respond to the changing needs of these community schools. For example, during the Gulf War, when the Yemeni minibus was attacked by racists as it took students to the twilight Arabic sessions, we were able, quite easily, to switch the times of the classes to safer daylight hours at the weekends. We were also able to organise a day's in-service session for our teachers, tutored by the Yemeni language school teachers, on the impact of the war upon our students. All this activity and linking serves to enhance the understanding, profile and status of the languages of the local black communities, counters linguistic racism within and without the school—and makes these languages a normal, accepted, developmental and increasingly prestigious part of the curriculum and mainstream life of the inner city school.

Similarly, when our school was threatened with closure by the local education authority, the force of the local languages added weightily to the campaign to save the school and became a formidable force to be reckoned with. The powerful persuasion of the organisers, teachers and students of the language classes accommodated at the school, plus school students and parents, asserted their will to keep the school open with their own words expressed through their banners and slogans. Defiant words of Urdu, Arabic and Somali were held up to the sky over the heads of demonstrators when LEA officers and councillors visited the at pickets outside the school during the period of the campaign. The communities' languages were in full colour and cry, and helped to win the campaign and ensure a future for the school.

Languages and Unity
Speak up, speak up, don't be scared!
Shout loud don't be sad!

Be proud.
This is your language.
Make them hear and feel and fear.
Make them feel what you are feeling,
Don't be afraid, I am here!
Don't feel what they are feeling
Shout loud, make them hear!
Speak loud, don't be afraid, this is your language.
That's why you are here.

Jameela Musaid (14)

Such words as these—written about the Arabic language by a Yemeni girl in Sheffield, but inspired by a poem by an Urdu poet of Pakistan and a schoolboy poet of East London writing in English—express the power and hugeness of languages, but also their essential unity. The sharing of language through the students' own far-flung words and the words of translation bring a profound richness and breadth to the pedagogy of the inner-city classroom. Our students, for example, are able to read, recite and understand some of the great poetry of our century in their own languages, and those who don't understand them directly can still appreciate and read their beauty and insights through translations, sometimes made by their classmates themselves.

One such poem, in Urdu, by the great Pakistani poet Faiz Ahmad Faiz, is the simple and striking *Speak*.[7] A class of ninth year students wrote their own responses to this poem. A Pakistani boy saw the immediacy of the message by his own national poet, and wrote the following:

What Language means to me

Speak the language that you were born with,
Show your feelings to the people around you.
Show the people you are proud of your language,
Language is a great thing.
With language you can make friends.
People will know you as long as you live,
Language can help you understand things around you
Language can make you proud and happy.
Language will lead you to happiness.
Don't let anyone make fun of your language
Shout your language out to the people around you!
Let them know that you love your language
And you will speak your language as long as you live
So shout your language out!

Izat (14)

What Izat writes is for all languages, and the inner-city classroom becomes their workshop and theatre. Responding to the same Faiz poem, Khadeegha from Syria saw her own first language as her as her life and hope.

My Arabic Language

Words of my language are expressive and dear to me.
That's how I feel about my language
No matter how far I go
No matter where I go
I'll still think of my precious language.
Some people think that a language
Is something that is just spoken.
It is in a way
But there is more to it.
It's something
that is very precious,
It's something
that a person is born with,
It's something
that I would never swap,
It's something
that can't be destroyed,
It's something
That is all yours and the people around you.
My language
My heart is throbbing
My heart starts to beat more
when my language is mentioned,
I think of me
and what I am going to do.
My language might give me work?
A home?
a good education?

That's what I will always hope for
and dream of.

I hope it will come true one day.

It was not only the black students who were prompted to react so strongly to Faiz' poem. The power of his language in translation deeply affected their white classmates. One of them, James, saw his opportunity to assert the power of his own Sheffield life and speech. Far from provoking him towards hostile or racist language, he spoke and wrote proudly of his own community and himself. When he read his statement to the class, it was strongly appreciated and understood by the black students, themselves Sheffielders, precisely because they understood his passion—like he had understood theirs:

I'm Proud to Speak!

I speak English, because I was born in England. I am proud to be English. I speak for freedom, and rights, against pollution and to make Sheffield a better city.

I speak about the World Student Games and the regeneration of Sheffield.

But in England many people have different accents like Geordies, Londoners, and Liverpudlians.

I speak a lot because it is something that I am good at.

I communicate with people by speaking. If I did not speak, how could I express my feelings, my hurt, anger, happiness, sadness and how could I tell anyone that I have a problem? How could they tell me the answer? How could the teachers at school teach me?

As soon as I was born. I heard voices, Yorkshire voices. So I learned the Yorkshire accent. I grew up in Yorkshire so I speak in my own accent.

So that's why I'm proud to speak!

James' piece was an important one. It showed how British working class speech must hold its own with the orchestra of languages which now sounds in British inner-city schools. For although a mastery of Standard English remains the strongest unifying linguistic factor for all our students, the history, poetry and experience contained within the dialects of the British working class must still be succoured and developed alongside all the other first languages of all the communities using the schools. In this way the use of language as a racist weapon is defeated, and it works becoming a message and tool of friendship.

This was certainly true of Nadia's fine poem, which follows. As a part of a study of the Palestinian people, the same ninth year class read poems in Arabic and English translations by Palestinian poets Samih al-Qasim and Mahmoud Darwish.[8] They expressed a cutting oppression, the pain of subjection and the force of imagination and hope. Darwish's poem *Identity card*[9] made a telling impression on the Arabic-speaking children in the class, who felt so close to the suffering of the Palestinians. Nadia, from a local Yemeni family, entered their experience in this extraordinary message of empathy.

Life-Land

It was a normal day
A normal morning
And a normal unhappy feeling.

I went to a market

To buy all I can afford
For my family,
When a man dressed
In a green suit
A cap
And carrying a rifle
(And that made him a soldier,
And that gave him the right to order me around!)
Suddenly stopped me with his rifle.
He pointed it at me,
Asking me where is my identity card?
Identity? We are the Palestinians!
We were born free
In our fathers' and grandfathers' land called Palestine—
The Holy Land.

We have our identity
Not just in Palestine but through the whole world,
And it destroys the happiness and the joy which is in our
hearts
And it destroys-our children too!
The children,
Children who don't have freedom any more
They don't have a future to enjoy
They don't have a future to finish their education.
They want to build their future
But deep, deep inside
They know the Israelis won't give them a chance.
It is all right for the Israeli children,
They have the right
Yes, they have the right to be free
And to have a bright future—
Because they have a life-land,
A land which is not taken over by other people.

Our children
As soon as they learn to walk,
They need to learn how to carry a weapon!
They have to
Our children,
They would love to go to school
And to hold a pen and pencil like other children
around the world

After all we are all the same
But nobody, nobody will give them a chance.
And we cry
Cry for all the world—
Cry for the Israeli government
To give us our freedom and our country.
You know the Israeli system—
Why, why do they treat us like this?

Democracy, democracy is just for Israelis
Palestinians are not included.
In the name of Allah,
We don't ask much from the Israeli government,
But just for all the Palestinians
To be free and to live like everyone else in the world,
To be with our families
To sleep in our homes in peace
And to hope for a glorious morning!

Nadia Saleh

For Nablus, Jerusalem and Ramallah are not so far from the top of a bus in Attercliffe, Sheffield, if you are an Arab. The so-called 'Gypsy Languages' too, have many variants and a spectrum of beauty and strength which is a part of the treasure of our inner-city classrooms and the communities which come together to learn inside them, to create new words and sentences—and develop a culture where racism has no place.

Notes

1   See *Deadly Silence: black deaths in custody*, Institute of Race Relations, London 1991
2   Searle, Chris and Shaif, Abdulgalil, *'Drinking from one pot'*, Yemeni unity, at home and overseas', *Race and Class*, April-June 1991, London
3   For a detailed account of racism in the *Sun*, see Searle, Chris, *Your Daily Dose: Racism and the Sun,* Campaign for Press and Broadcasting Freedom. London 1989
4   *Your Daily Dose*, op. cit.
5   See Linguistic Minorities Project, *The Other Languages of England*, Routledge and Kegan Paul, London 1985
6   *Struggle for Language: Voluntary Language Classes in Sheffield*, a report by Shaif, Abdulgalil for Sheffield Education Committee, SUMES, Sheffield 1989
7   See the poetry collection *One for Blair*, Edited by Searle, Chris, Young World Books, London 1989
8   Poems by Samih al-Qasim and Mahmoud Darwish can be found in *Victims of a Map*, Al Saqi Books, London, 1984
9   See Mahmoud-Darwish, *The Music of Human Flesh*, Poems of the Palestinian Struggle, Heinemann, London 1980

THE GULF BETWEEN: A SCHOOL AND A WAR   (1991)

I want to concentrate upon the impact of the Gulf war of 1991 on the lives of our students, and on our school itself as a living institution—but in doing this, I am all the time conscious of a certain irony in using the word 'gulf'.

For, in curriculum terms and within the scope of what we teach and learn, throughout this war there was another 'gulf'—if not an abyss. The war not only presented to us issues about internal school relationships, the pressure upon unity and the school's attitude to the communities which it serves. Over and above these crucial aspects was the school's function as a formulator and conductor of knowledge itself, and the gulf over which it stood between two versions of knowledge, two registers of assumed fact, that were in currency all around and through the school, its neighbourhood and communities.

On the one hand, there was a state-licensed, state-approved stratum of knowledge. This was one track in its perspective, national-chauvinist in its orientation, anti-Arab, anti-internationalist, and largely prevalent in the public consciousness outside the school. It was formed through television, tabloid newspapers, the positions (and consensus) of government and mainline 'opposition', and squared with the ideology set down in the 'National Curriculum' currently being imposed on all British schools. On the other hand, there was a view that was organic and critical, arising from the real lives of the students at school—in particular the Arab students, for many of whom internationalism was a necessary aspect of their lives, having either been brought up in the Middle East, in countries like Yemen, Syria or Jordan, or having been for long family sojourns there. This view was grounded in a community's real knowledge of life and its struggles, in a living understanding of the importance of the economy and the effects of oil imperialism.

There is no doubt that in many British schools the Gulf war had a damaging and divisive impact. Schools with all-white student populations often found themselves, almost automatically, because of force of culture, nationalism and the imperial legacy, taking active sides with British and US political and military objectives and strategies. These schools became the domestic cheerleaders for the allied war efforts, giving jingoistic support for 'our boys', the new crusaders of the Gulf, with mass letter-writing to the troops, parcel-sending, fund-raising and other such publicity exercises.

For other schools, composed of black and white British cohorts, a potentially more volatile situation emerged, with Pakistani and Bangladeshi students often supporting Saddam Hussein (whom many even saw as an authentic Islamic hero) while the white students retained an uncritical loyalty to the British military intervention. Sometimes inter-communal bitterness and violence broke out, both in and out of school.

While some of these schools futilely tried to press down the lid on their students' responses—some even forbidding classroom discussion and debate about the war—others took what they saw as a neutral and objective line, while still defending the allied position. The largest and most progressive British teachers' union, the National Union of Teachers, took a cautious approach in its 'advice' leaflet, 'Gulf war: the impact on schools'. This argued that 'it may be helpful to hold discussions about conflict resolutions whilst in no way seeking to influence the beliefs of individuals about the rightness or justice of the war. This would not be in keeping with the Union's long held belief in education for peace.'

A few other schools set out to create a spirit of genuine openness and discourse, while unashamedly standing up for peace and for a solution to be found by the Arab peoples themselves. The account that follows sets down the processes of response to the war in one such comprehensive school in Sheffield.

I write as the school's headteacher, but also as an active English teacher. The students all live in the neighbourhood of the school, a working-class district close to the industrial end of the city, where its once-great steel industry was located. With just under half the students from local white families, the others come from Pakistani, Yemeni, Somali and Caribbean communities. One of the school's teachers is an exiled Iraqi.

During the days before the war, and as the two huge armies face each other across the desert with the UN deadline approaching hour by hour, there is a fear and uncertainty among the students. Many of them can sense the scale and conflict of the events about to unfold. Many of them write down their reflections and read them out to each other in their English class. Some of these are marked not only by their honesty but by a sense of being overpowered by huge, uncontrollable issues which they cannot fully understand. One 12 year old boy, Lee, writes:

> I do not think that Britain and the UN should go to war against Iraq because it would mean a lot of people would die, including people who are not soldiers. Iraq says that they are taking back land which already belongs to them and which the British took away from them ...
>
> Some people say that America only wants to protect Kuwait because of the oil in the area, which is bought by other western countries.
>
> The environmental impact of a war in the Gulf would last for many, many years, causing further destruction of the ozone layer which would have a disastrous effect on everyone all over the world.
>
> There are many issues involved when discussing the Gulf crisis and some of these I don't understand. This makes the question 'Should Britain go to war with Iraq?' very difficult to answer. But I would like to see a peaceful solution to the matter.

Jackleen, a 15 year old Yemeni girl who has only been in Britain for five months, is also tentative, but from a completely different perspective and exploring the contradictions she sees all around her:

> I don't know what I can say about this problem. Really it is a big problem because we do not know what will happen.
>
> I really don't like the war and every one I know doesn't like the war. Why the war, why? I get in my head more questions about this problem, I know I don't agree with anyone ... but this doesn't mean I don't like the leader.
>
> Why when Israel went to Palestine did no one do anything, it's just all countries said, 'It's not my problem, it is a Palestine problem.' Why does no country care about the Palestine problem? And same things in Afghanistan, why and why and why?? In this letter I want to ask America, England and all countries why, in an Arab area, have these countries come to help Kuwait?
>
> I know some people from America and England don't like the war and don't want to go to Kuwait to fight because it is not their country ... but the heads of state want to help Kuwait not only because they love Kuwait, not all this, it's because they want *oil*. I am sorry if I said this ... but this is all in my head.
>
> I don't like the war so please leave the Arabic countries to solve this problem themselves. I really want to see all Arabic countries working together, not like as they do now.

And contradictions there are, rising all around our students. In the recently unified Yemen, many of their families are suffering the direct consequences of their government's neutrality and its refusal to support the US/British/Saudi military alliance against Iraq. The Saudi government has expelled nearly a million Yemeni migrant workers, and their remittances are no longer there to boost the national economy and provide a financial base for thousands of dependent Yemeni families. On the other side of the frontier, one of our fourth-year students, Abdullah, on an extended visit to his family in Jeddah, had been conscripted into the Saudi army. Abdullah is a tall, burly youth who looks much older than his fifteen years, and his uncle came to the school, seeking help to get him back to Britain. We wrote to the Saudi authorities asking them to secure his release from military service and allow him to continue his education with us. He came back just before the war began, beaming all over his face as he walked back into school. Now he laughs and fools around with his Yemeni classmates, who are obviously glad to see him.' In Saudi when we dig in the sand, we find oil', he jokes. 'Not like you Yemenis. When you dig, all you find is dirty water!' The Yemenis, taking all this in good humour, seem to have the final laugh. 'He's a Yemeni like us, we know his family. His father now lives in Saudi so he thinks he's Saudi too.'

For some of the other students there is also a closeness to the war. A Pakistani girl, Majida, writes: 'I don't want the war to go on because my friend's dad has been to the

war and this time he will have to go again. If he doesn't go he will be under arrest.'
Brian. in his second-year class, also seems affected by the call-up of British military
reservists, in the heart of his family. He sets down:

> Another reason why I don't want the war to start is because my Dad and
> my brothers will have to go back in the army, and they might get hurt and
> maybe get killed.

You would think that such opposing loyalties would polarise these young people.
Everything around them is persuading them to take sides simplistically and emotionally:
religion, national chauvinism, family connections, plus the media bombardment in the
tabloid press, particularly the Murdoch press and the *Sun*. Morning after morning come
the banner headlines pouring hatred and scorn on the Iraqi people. 'We'll bomb them
till they drop' screams the *Sun* on 31 January. In the local daily, the *Sheffield Star*, there
are photographs of schoolgirls up against the Union Jack, raising money to send gifts
to British troops in the Gulf, and a story about another girl writing to the soldiers who
have 'gone to the Gulf to fight for the Queen and our country'.' Whose country? The
Guardian publishes an article about an 11 year old schoolgirl at Falia Park Primary
School near Gateshead. She wrote a poem about Saddam Hussein that was published
in the local newspaper, the *Gateshead Post*, after a local group of the Territorial Army
sent it in to them. It goes like this:

> Saddam Hussein is the man we hate
> We'll get him 'just you wait!
> He's trying to take over, get him out,
> 'He doesn't belong there', we'll all shout.
> We'll take his head and mash it up
> Until it fits into an egg cup,
> Take off his arms, take off his legs
> Bend them back until he begs.
> Take his head, take his heart
> Rip the stupid man apart,
> Poke out his eyes, chew off his nose
> Kick him in the head, pull off his toes.

Reading these published words, this sadism from one so young, I suddenly understand
again something so horrific, residual, still there throbbing in the British and European
mind towards the Arab peoples, welling out of their imperial past. I am reminded of the
'Crusades', the siege of Ma'arra in 1098, and how European historians themselves
wrote how 'in Ma'arra our troops boiled pagan adults in cooking pots; they impaled
children on spits and devoured them grilled'.[3] Or, closer to our own time, in the Yemen
in 1967, of the Argyll soldiers and their inter-platoon rivalry in Aden, and how Robertson

Jam golliwog stickers were awarded to an officer whose soldiers succeeded in killing an Arab. One officer had admitted:

> At one stage my platoon had notched up 13 kills and another platoon were one kill behind. The corporal even told the private he was to use his bayonet, for it was to be that kind of killing.
>
> They went into an alley and killed a young Arab who was out after curfew.[4]

Yet, in the midst of this historical and present hatred, our young people could keep their minds level, remember their schoolmates and friendships and still resist division. One 14 year old Pakistani girl, Shazia, wrote:

> Soldiers are fighting for oil. People are dying because of this war. Innocent lives are involved in this crisis. People in Iraq and Saudi Arabia are all scared because of this war. President Bush and Saddam Hussein do not think about people, soldiers and their families. They just want the oil. When people ask me, 'which side are you on?', I say I did not want this war to happen in the first place. But it has. But I am on no one's side. I want it to end. I do not want it to become a world war just because of oil.

During the first week of the war, while British, American and Saudi aircraft are bombing Iraq and the sorties go into their thousands, we hold year assemblies on the subject of the war. The objective is to formalise the dialogue going on between the students at the playground and classroom level, to hold their views together, and create more mutual understanding within the framework of peace. Of course there are differences which come across strongly in these assemblies. Corin, a 14 year old white boy, makes these points out loud:

> Even though war is a horrible occurrence, sometimes it can't be helped. People being killed isn't a pleasant thing, but when someone just walks into a country and tries to take it over, something has to be done about it. Different people have different views, like some say England and America should mind their own business. I think this is true, but Kuwait asked the help of England and America, so I think they should stay where they are.
>
> Other views are that England are only in Kuwait because it's full with oil. This may be true, but why is Saddam Hussein in there? It can't just be that Kuwait used to be a part of Iraq, because what's the point in fighting for a bit of land unless you get something out of it at the end?

Nadia, his Yemeni classmate, gives her reply with all her year listening:

> I don't think Britain should go to war with Iraq because it would be very dangerous and it would affect the whole world, It was very dangerous for the Americans and British to get involved in the Gulf crisis! The Arabs should talk about it and sort everything out between themselves.

Very innocent people will get killed around the world, especially in the Arab countries. The Americans and British are only in Saudi Arabia because they know that Fahad would give them something, e.g., oil, land.

Why didn't the Americans and British go to help Palestine? In my opinion, I think the Americans and British didn't help Palestine because it is a poor country.

The Americans and British would not like the Arabs to interfere with them!

The question of Palestine was often at the centre of the students' arguments. This year group has recently been studying the intifada and the lives of Palestinians on the West Bank, and several of the students have written letters to young Palestinians in a school in Ramallah, with the intention of setting up a permanent link between our two schools. 'Why don't they [the British and Americans] stop Israelis taking over Palestine?' protests one Pakistani boy in his essay on the war, while another Yemeni boy answers the question: 'The Palestinians are not rich and they have got no oil.' In a similar vein, James, a classmate of Corin and Nadia, adds: 'But why should we have to fight? Why should we be greedy, and have all the oil. The consequences will be dreadful.' And, with strong insights on the same question and her mind on the Al-Sabah ruling dynasty of Kuwait, 13 year old Haifa from the Yemen writes:

No, I think that Britain should not go to war against Iraq because it is an Arab people's matter and the matter should be solved between Arab countries ... The British people should take care of their own people not send them to battlefields as mercenaries, fighting to bring back one family to rule a country because that family is under the influence of the British government.

At a second-year assembly, spontaneous applause by almost all those present breaks out when Nicola, a 13 year old white girl, reads her thoughts to all her year-mates. Muslim and Christian backgrounds, national origins, race and culture all seem in agreement and to be at one when she reaches her final suggestion.

No!

Just simply no!

Britain should not go to war against Iraq. It's all Mr. Bush's fault. If they hadn't roped Mr. Major into sending forces, it would be all right.

On TV last week, two wards at a hospital had to be closed down because two paramedics had to go on stand-by in the Gulf. Just think about all those people missing medical treatment.

Saddam Hussein and Mr. Bush should talk about what they're going to do about this war and leave everybody else out of it. Bring everyone home from the Gulf and re-unite them with their families! And if Mr. Bush and Saddam Hussein can't make up their minds, we should let them fight it out themselves.

As the aerial bombardment of Iraq continues during the first three weeks of the war, the students continue to discuss and write about its meanings and implications. For the teachers, these raids have a special resonance. Our Arabic teacher, a much-liked colleague, is an Iraqi. His parents live in the neighbourhood of the bunker in Baghdad that is destroyed with a terrible loss of life. The war comes into our staff room too. Daily news bulletins are shown in the lunch hours in the Resources Area of the school, where national and local newspapers, from the Conservative *Daily Telegraph* to the Communist *Morning Star*, are also on display. Yemeni students also bring in Arabic newspapers, and often lunch hour sessions are full with watchers, readers and talkers, all concerned with the latest situation in the Gulf. We find some enthusiastic graffiti about Saddam on the wall in a languages room, and there is a couple of pro-Saddam slogans in the boys' main toilets. But while there is frequent discourse and open discussion about the war, there are no fights or violent arguments, and no evidence of jingoism, warlike talk and antipathy towards either Islamic or white British students.

The war, ironically, has become a stimulus for those students struggling to learn English as a second language. This is particularly true for the Arab language students, for they feel a deep urgency and real motivation to express their views to their English peers across the school. Safa has been in Britain for only five months before the start of the war. Yet the passion and poetry of her beginner's English produces its own form of eloquence.

> No one can go to an Arab country to protect it unless they want something from this country. But it's always Saddam's fault because he can't take Kuwait from its people and get them out from their country. And I think they have to look for a good idea for them all. I think the good idea is that Saddam has to get out from Kuwait. I think this is the best idea for them all because we don't want war and we don't need it, because war is the worst thing in the world. Because it burns everything, it will make the world very bad and thousands and thousands of people will be killed, and the animals and everything. It will kill the smile on the lips and make everything look bad.

For Samieh, another newly-arrived Yemeni, there are so many questions about his Arab people and those who are interfering with their lives. It is the forming of such questions and the finding of answers to them that will bring him the language he is learning so quickly as well as the truth for which he craves.

> As I heard in ITN news that President Saddam Hussein has attacked Kuwait because he thinks that Kuwait is a part of his country. I have seen, too, many people on the television shouting 'we do not want war', and I have also heard children saying 'why do we, the children, always have to bear the costs?'. Why don't Mr. Bush and Mr. Major the prime minister of the United Kingdom, why don't they bear the costs why, why and why? ...

And I also heard an old man saying why don't Mr. Saddam Hussein and Mr. Bush and Mr. Major the prime minister of the United Kingdom solve this out with peace and without any war? Why does Mr. Bush want to help Kuwait for the oil, and this oil will destroy our and their armies and their nation and our friends, and they have got nothing to do with these problems? Why don't they solve the problems in the Middle East, since 1967? I will answer this question, because in the Middle East, which includes Palestine, the Palestinians are not rich and they have got no oil.

I am saying this especially to Mr. Bush and Mr. Major to do nothing about themselves. Nothing will happen to them because they are in England and the USA. Think about the Arab countries and about what will happen in Yemen or in Iraq or in Kuwait or in Saudi Arabia. I like to say these words, and I am saying this especially to Mr. Bush and Mr. Major, who do not think about them since nothing will happen to them ... Think about what will happen in Yemen or in Iraq or in Kuwait or in Saudi Arabia. I like to say these words ...

And I am saying to Mr Saddam Hussein, please do think about what will happen to him and his army.

If there will be a very long war I am ready to give my life and my blood to protect my Arab countries and my Arab families. I am ready to give my life and my body to save the truth.

God will be with the truth.

As students like Samieh work out their thoughts, and go to the computers to project them on screens and bring them out, the questions they raise are about subjection, imperialism, national liberation and economic independence. In their own words, they are dealing with these complex issues, and their English-born peers are listening to them and learning from them. The same questions are being put in the form of poems, and answers, too, emerge that are being shared by everyone. Mohammed Kassim asks:

Why is the world always in war?
Why do the rich hate the poor?
Why can't the whiteman love the blackman?
Why can't they be friends, what don't they like?

But there were powers behind these questions.

But no
They want to rule what is not theirs
They make excuses and support millionaires.
If only they could stop and think on their demands
Maybe war would stop and they could shake hands.
Peace could stop killing in the sand.
Peace could remove the gun from the hand.
Solidarity is the way we should live today
And together as one we should stand up for our say.

There could hardly be poetic thoughts so different from those of the girl in Gateshead. We manage to persuade a Sheffield local paper to publish Mohammed Kassim's poem too. The truth is that the presence of such a highly-motivated and clear-thinking cohort of students in our school as those from the Yemeni community has a genuine impact on the thinking of many other students. The Yemeni community has its own school: it organises its classes three evenings a week in our school buildings, regularly attracting over a hundred students to each session. It is voluntary, being completely organised by and through the community's contacts and infrastructures. It teaches Arabic, Yemeni history and culture, Islamic studies, and 'manners'— or how to treat other people. All this has a dynamic effect on the mainstream daily classes in our school.

Then, in the middle of the war period, some stone-throwing racist whites attack the Yemeni Community Association minibus as it brings a group of children to the evening classes. The community has already felt the lash of other racist acts—abusive telephone calls, insults in the street and graffiti scrawled over their community centre—but the attack on the minibus is particularly dangerous, it could have caused serious injury, or worse, to the children. When the community asks whether the classes can be switched to weekend daylight hours to make attacks less likely, the school immediately agrees, and also asks whether some Yemeni speakers could conduct an in-service session for our entire teaching staff on the history of the community in Sheffield, its links to the homeland and its response to the Gulf.

This is a very productive session, and is pivotal in helping to raise the understanding of all our teachers. The film, *Thank you, that's all I know,*[5] by Christine Bellamy, which describes the history and struggles of Sheffield's Yemenis, is shown. It includes some grim footage of British colonial brutality in Aden, and the rounding up and mistreatment of Yemenis on the streets of the city which is a revelation to some of the teachers. There is also an explanation of the literacy campaign being run from within the Yemeni community, delivered by one of its young women teaching assistants. Mohammed Kassim, himself a fifth-year student at our school, addresses his teachers and describes the curriculum and organisation of the community language school. What also comes out of the session is the realisation that one of our black colleagues, Owen (a Barbadian), had served as ground crew in the Royal Air Force for two years in Aden, in the early 1960s. In an interview, recorded later, with two Yemeni sixteen-year-olds, he tells them of his experiences as a part of the British occupying force during the years of the Aden insurrection. He recalls how the British officers prevented the black servicemen from mixing with the Arab population in case they showed sympathy for them, of the friendliness found during the times they did mix, and of the racist barriers in the British armed forces that stopped him, or any other black recruit he knew, from achieving promotion,

'Think of all the people that are going to be killed. Don't just think about yourself, think about other people in the world, they may be in the war while we are England.'

This message, written at the beginning of the conflict by Azra, a second-year Pakistani girl, becomes even more truthful by its end. International Women's Day falls during the week following the ceasefire and among the visitors and speakers who come to the school to commemorate it is Jenny Hales, an elderly peace campaigner who lives in the neighbourhood of the school. Speaking on the theme of 'Women and Peace', she tells how she had been a member of the international peace mission that camped on the Kuwaiti/Saudi border, between the opposing armies, at the outset of the long stand-to before the war. She speaks of the Iraqi soldiers who were guarding the camp, and how they and the campaigners opened up their lives to each other during the cool desert evenings. She tells of the horror and betrayal that she felt when the allied bombers first flew overhead to bomb Baghdad, and describes how, when the campaigners were evacuated to Baghdad, the Iraqis there, even though her countrymen were flying the planes that were causing such death and destruction, approached them with warmth and friendship.

Jenny Hales's talk has a strong effect on many of her listeners, and, as she speaks, she shows them the awesome photograph of an incinerated Iraqi soldier that has been published in the *Observer* the previous Sunday, above the headline 'The real face of war'.' This one, terrible image of the carnage which followed the massacre of the retreating Iraqis on the Basra road during the last hours of the 'ground war', shocks and stays with many of the students. This is the 'enemy' that the triumphing allied commanders and their men have so roundly vanquished. During their English lesson the next day I suggest they write down the last thoughts of this Iraqi soldier.

Nadia begins in this way, with the soldier looking for a 'sense of peace':

> My wife I'll be back.
> Please don't grieve, I'll be back,
> Son, I'll be back,
> No, don't cry.
>
> I'm on my way home.
> Mother and Father
> Do not weep.
> Soon I will be home, to keep you strong.
> I'll bring money, food and clothes.
> We shall build a house,
> Or even own a car.
>
> Do not worry,
> The war is nearly settled,
> So, do not weep!

Marie, a white classmate, seems to find a kind of freedom in his mind:

> Free at last,
> Free from the danger
> Of shooting guns,
> Free from the danger
> Of whistling missiles,
> Free from the guilt
> Of what has been forced upon me.
>
> I'll see my family soon,
> Not to mention my friends.
> I hope they don't ask questions,
> I don't want to live through pain again,
> Tomorrow cannot come too soon.

While a Pakistani student, Izat, creates three lines that hold a whole war within them:

> I can hear a voice of oil burning
> Back in Iraq there are people crying for food and yearning
> I want this war to end.

But perhaps the most moving response is from Safa again—now a few war weeks further on in her learning of English. For her soldier it is only his family that matters, and in particular his brother whom he protects and loves as a parent.

My last thoughts

My little brother Saleh I am coming back to you as soon as this war has finished. I want to stay beside you, feeding you and giving you everything you want. I'll give you your books, pens to learn how to write and read. I will get you clothes for school, and new clothes for Eid.

Don't worry brother, I'm your father and mother and everything. I will stay near you and keep looking after you to protect you.

I will do all these things when I come back.

I want you to grow up and be a doctor or a soldier and anything good that you want to be. But I want you to remember your country and how to build it to be a prosperous country. I wish I could do all these things if I came back to you, if not, God will be with you.

Perhaps some people are happy and their families are around them, but I know for others they are not.

I don't want you to cry. I want you to be a man, a strong man to feed yourself and look after yourself if I don't come back. I want you to be the best, not for me but for yourself first, and for your country second.

I want you to know that I don't want to kill anybody, for we are not animals, we are people.

I don't want you to forget this. I want you to remember it all your life. I am dreaming, and I wish to do all these things when I come back.

Afterword

Just as the war ended, another, different one began for the school. The local education department, as a part of its efforts to cut back its general schools budget, announced that either our school, or a neighbouring comprehensive school on an almost all-white working class estate, would have to be closed. This appalling decision virtually pitched the two schools against each other in a battle for survival: one would be the winner, the other the loser. Both schools resisted this pressure to fight it out, and embarked upon a unified campaign for joint survival, but the danger for both communities, in the potential loss of their main local education resource, was real. For what kind of system was it that could spend 14 million daily on sustaining an interventionist war on another continent, and close its schools at home?

For us, the unity, made stronger by the weeks of the war, remained precious as we went into our campaign to save the school. As Shameem, a third-year Pakistani girl, wrote in her campaign poem which we published in our parents newsletter (in an obvious rhyme that no one had discovered before):

> Asians, Somalis, Saudis, Syrians, English and Yemenis -
> We all come to this school and we're not enemies.

And her classmate Elizabeth reinforced this same message in another unifying image:

> I don't want this school to close. Here I feel I've known everyone since I was small. We are all a family, teachers and children, black and white. It doesn't matter who you are. If you are in our school you are part of this family. There may be war in the world, but at our school we are at peace with each other.

As these new campaigns began, two fifth-year girls came to my office with an idea which had gripped them. One was Sawsan, a Jordanian, the other her white English friend Kay. They spoke of some Iraqi families that Sawson has got to know. Unsupported by their own government, and not qualifying for any assistance from the British social services, they had no money at all. The next day, the girls brought in an Iraqi mother and, while her child played among the books in my office, she explained how her husband—a medical student—was now without his scholarship, and how the family had been left financially stranded. The girls decided to organise a series of fund raising events for these families, and began with a sponsored lunch for the teachers.

This lunch had some publicity on the local paper, and the same evening Sawsan received a threatening, anonymous phone call, promising 'acid in your face' if she continued to raise money for Iraqis, plus a battery of racist insults. Frightened, but undaunted, the girls carried on.

Two weeks later, after the first payments had been made to the families from the money that the girls had raised, Sawsan bought in a beautiful hand-sewn tapestry, made by the Iraqi mother who had visited us. It was a gift for the school. Across the black fabric and written in Arabic in golden sequins, was a verse from the Koran, praising human unity and the God of the daybreak.

Notes

1   *The Star*, Sheffield, 12 February 1991.
2   Andrew Moncur's Diary, *Guardian*, 7 February 1991.
3   Amin Maalouf, *The Crusades through Arab Eyes*, London 1984.
4   'The Aden File', *Sunday Mail*, 17 May 1981
5   *Thank you, that's all I know*, a film by Christine Bellamy, Sheffield Film Co-op, 1990.
6   *Observer*, 3 March 1991

'ONLY A PENCIL': THE CENTRALITY OF LITERACY   (1992)

The word 'literacy' is not commonly used within the context of British schools. As a term it has been much more widely adopted by adult educators than schoolteachers. And yet, at almost any period in the history of modern education worldwide—with the exceptions of those eras of revolutionary upheaval in nations of vast populations which have been mobilised for largescale campaigns of mass adult literacy, such as in the Soviet Union, China or Ethiopia—the majority of people learning how to read and write in the world have been children studying in their schools.

It is important to remember this, otherwise we shall see 'literacy' generally as a process in which adults involve themselves, while children are engaged in a different form of learning about language and experience—something which certainly involves them in learning how to read and write, but something which cannot be called 'literacy' because it happens early in life, as if it happens 'when it should', as a part of the sequence of civilised and 'normal' human social development. To be part of a 'literacy' programme or process however, is almost certainly to be seen as working in an adult context, learning in a compensatory mode, making up for that which was either lost or not on offer when the student was of school age—as something exceptional and special, rather then as a routine activity that corresponds to a phase of 'natural' development.

There may be many reasons for these misconceptions, but one of them certainly is the value that 'literacy' (if we mean mass and campaigning approaches to adult literacy, such as those initiatives connected with radical educators like Paulo Freire[1] or national liberation movements and anti-imperialist governments such as those in Cuba, Nicaragua, Vietnam, Guinea-Bissau or Chile) puts upon transforming *consciousness*, and in particular social and political consciousness.

For whereas such consciousness may be seen as part and parcel of progressive, modern literacy processes involving adults, 'teaching children to read and write'— whatever method being used, from phonetic approaches, 'look and say', the use of reading schemes to the so-called 'real books' method—is still largely viewed as a routine, unpolitical, non-consciousness raising process, just a phase of learning (albeit a vital one, seeing as there is so much controversy and heat about what is the 'best" method) of a child's state-organised primary education.

So there is 'literacy', which adult students do (although ironically, in mass campaigns as in Nicaragua and Ethiopia, schoolchildren are often the *teachers*[2]) and 'learning how to read and write', which child students do every day in their schools throughout the 'developed' world. The discomfort many schoolteachers of language may feel in considering what they do as teaching 'literacy' may well be connected to the implication that whereas 'teaching reading and writing' is simply and mechanically teaching the de-contextualised skills to achieve just and only that with a child, 'literacy' means going completely against the accepted grain of school life and culture, abandoning curriculum 'neutrality' and 'objectivity' and concerning oneself with the 'adults only' ingredient of raising consciousness through the selection of 'provocative' or 'propagandist' content or contexts.

Literacy and School

As a teacher of English in the British state school system of education, I, and many other teachers, have always challenged this apparent consensus of 'neutrality' of language teaching and curriculum. In other state systems of education where I have taught and contributed—such as those in Mozambique, Grenada and Ethiopia—there have been foundations based upon revolutionary transformations in state power and the subsequent re-ordering of state educational provision. In such contexts, this neutrality concept—bogus as it has always proved to be in Britain—has been either swiftly or progressively abandoned and replaced by an alternative structure and a declared ideological and practical determination to support the cause and advance of the working people and the peasantry.

In 1975, in the introduction to my book *Classrooms of Resistance*[3], I wrote as a young teacher in East London that 'working class children should learn to read, write, spell, punctuate, to develop the word as a weapon and tool in the inevitable struggles for improvement and liberation for them, and the rest of their class all over the world.' To me, this was what 'literacy' was all about. Nothing in my subsequent educational experiences, from teaching in post-independence Mozambique, leading an innovative teacher education programme in revolutionary Grenada to now being a headteacher in a British inner-city comprehensive school, has made me change my mind on that statement and all its implications. The imperative task facing the language teacher, of ensuring that his or her students fully develop a knowledge, understanding and ability to use to their full the language resources they will need in their lives, still holds primacy over all other tasks, and has, indeed, never been so important as it is now. Yet to detach the social and political context of working class children's literacy from the skills that it involves for reasons of a spurious 'neutrality', has always been and continues to be as pedagogically crippling as it is politically and morally wrong. That children, like adults—as shown millions of times over by Freire in Brazil or by the literacy processes in Guinea-Bissau, Nicaragua, Ethiopia, Grenada or the struggling *barrios* of Mexico City or La Paz[4]—learn best when they read their own worlds as well as their own words, has also been demonstrated in the *schools* of those same countries countless times and continues to be the truth in British inner-city classrooms, or those holding children from oppressed and exploited sections of the population anywhere in the world where they learn. This is why the insights of mass literacy campaigns have always been as relevant to schoolchildren and their teachers as they are to adult learners and educators. Children can never be too young to use their skills-in-acquisition of literacy to confront, criticise or question, as well as to form their own rational attitudes to issues arising from their own world, whether it be the state of their school or street, the taxes or rents paid by their parents, the suffering or struggles of other human beings or life anywhere on their planet, or current questions of peace, war, consent or resistance. In all these areas and contexts of learning and teaching, skills and consciousness go hand-in-hand.

The Third Dimension

Yet there is another vital dimension, and that is the *imagination*—which can turn a moribund and static form of language learning into a vibrant, living literacy. In the poem that follows, a ten year old boy from a Sheffield primary school considers literacy—and in particular the tool of writing and learning, the pencil—from the imaginative perspective of an Ethiopian school student who has taken part in his nation's mass literacy campaign by teaching illiterate adults within his own family.[5] By this act of learning about learning through imaginative empathy, he brings forward new insights about the functions of literacy in his own life, as well as in another life thousands of miles away, and expands his own burgeoning use of words and ideas:

> **It's only a pencil**
> Here I am looking at something that holds my whole life.
> If I let it go my life will be gone.
> Not only my life, but my family's as well.
> But who cares? After all, it's only a pencil.
> It's only a pencil, but look what I can do with it.
> I can write a letter for help with it.
> I can learn at school with it.
> I can teach my family with it—
> If only we had more pencils and less guns.
>
> Joe Carlisle

'More pencils and less guns': within that new and discovered combination of reflection and words are unexpected meanings which stretch the poetry of a Yorkshire child writing in a Sheffield classroom to the crux of political tensions and inequalities across the entire world. Thus his achievement has centred upon the exercise of three developing areas of his education: skills, consciousness and the imagination, all essential components of a school literacy process and, in his case, all in balance and working in cooperation.

At this point we should consider what happens when these components get out of balance or become divorced from each other—or when undue emphasis is taken off one and put onto another. As I have already argued, the teaching of 'reading and writing' in schools, as opposed to the teaching of literacy in schools, has only rarely been concerned with the development of a critical consciousness among children. It was certainly a vehicle for teaching children to imbibe approved and establishment attitudes and consciousness, the ways of thinking and acting that were licensed and approved by the ruling interests in the state and the economy. These involved support for the *status quo*, for Empire, for King or Queen and country, and for its prevailing social, cultural and economic systems. The dozens of reading schemes and early childhood reading books give unending testimony to this unquestioning, consenting and uncritical child's reading universe, a cosmos of Empire and Britain that was implanted in the mind of the colonised child too, all over the world, as well as deeply into the psyche of the child of the British working class. This is what this child found herself in for generations through the books she had to read at school: the settled, cuddly middle class life of Janet and John, Peter and Jane, their families, cosy streets holidays by the seaside, their large gardens and dogs and cats—it was this world, always white and comfortable, that she was projected into by her school, no matter how little her actual life resembled this read and distant version of reality. It was this world that she had to exchange for her own when she entered the doors of the school reading curriculum.

Much of this stereotyped and regulated approach in Britain changed with the liberal and child-centred ideas of primary school education signalled by the 1967 'Plowden Report'.[6] This put the individual child, rather than children and their communities at the focal point of school life and curriculum. 'At the heart of the educational process is the child" declared the Report in its introductory passages. One result of this shift as manifested in the teaching of reading and writing was to move from an emphasis on 'sheer skills' towards 'sheer creativity' and self expression, which often damaged, further the opportunities for working class children becoming proficient readers and writers. For those children coming from homes or whole communities where parents were illiterate in English or spoke a language other than English, the de-emphasising of the skills dimension of literacy was even more serious and handicapping, particularly as throughout the seventies and much of the eighties there was a devaluation of Standard English as a common language currency. It became fashionable among some 'progressive' educationalists to portray Standard English as solely the language of 'suburbia' and therefore not applicable to the language needs of working class and black children—as much more stress was being put on the validity of regional and Creole dialects, 'mother tongues' and working class varieties of English as vehicles for language learning. Although much of this emphasis was valuable, according new recognition to the strength and founding power of the underlying first language, it too often threw the kernel of proficiency in the standard language out—with the reactionary cultural context it was wrapped inside.[7]

A New Complexity

The growing presence in the British inner-city classrooms throughout the seventies and eighties of potentially bilingual children of primary and secondary school age who were categorised as 'ESL' (English as a second language) learners, also caused more overall effort to be put towards 'literacy' teaching, although the very low number of bilingual teachers in schools made bilingual language teaching a rare, even though much wished-for, phenomenon. But this new situation throughout British inner-cities raised some key questions which questioning and radical teachers strove to answer for the sake of all their students—including those from the white working class who were also experiencing a lack of success in the learning of literacy—questions which went to the very heart of their pedagogy. Where does 'literacy' teaching stop (if it ever stops), and English, Language Arts, Humanities or whatever it happened to be called in particular schools, begin? Can there be a line of demarcation? And what about the situation, now increasingly usual (rather than uncommon or exceptional) in working class or inner-city schools, where those who are literate in basics as native English users—but with a very limited knowledge of the standard language—share classrooms and curriculum with those who are illiterate or semiliterate in the standard language or *any* variety of English? And where the historical language complexities governed by class difference, whereby children with dialectal and regional variants of English who have always had difficulties in coming to terms with Standard English, share school and learning with children with underlaid languages like Punjabi, Hindi, Bengali, Arabic, Somali, Turkish, Greek or the Caribbean Creole languages—how is a unified literacy strategy to be developed here? And where these same speakers pass through an informal peer learning phase of language when they speak the English of East London, Sheffield, Glasgow or Liverpool before they come to grips with the Standard English of their school curriculum (now increasingly taking the form of a narrow and uniform National Curriculum)[8]—how can the question of literacy in school be simply resolved by 'teaching then how to read and write' in the early years of primary education?

In such a complexity of language and learning situations, can teachers of language ever be free of the need and responsibility to teach literacy, as an integral part of language teaching itself? Then literacy, like education itself, becomes more than a school-long process—it becomes a life-long process too, and across the entire curriculum of the school, not just in 'Language' or 'English' lessons. A part of the answer to such questions must be to envisage the advance of literacy in the British inner-city classroom as a dialogue, a communal learning act—not only in the sense of a cooperative, life-exchanging process between teacher and student, but even more importantly, a communion between the student body, between the minds, skills and imaginations that make up the cohort of the classroom in all 'subject' areas. These individuals add up to a combination of separate communities, interweaving histories and interdependent cultures and nations all gathered for the tasks of learning, yet all starting from variously and pointedly different points of arrival—linguistically, as in many other dimensions. Thus schools must take a central responsibility of bringing cohesion and unity to a heterogeneous community—to move away from the context of solely serving the individual child to serving the entire community of learners. And to change the maxim quoted earlier from the 'Plowden Report', 'At the centre of the educational process is the school: at the heart of the school is the community.'

A Communality of Peace

The spinal cord of this communal dialogue must be a commitment to *peace*, in both its detailed affirmation in questions of human activity between individuals from different communities learning together in the same school, and its wider and principled application to social justice, cooperation and friendship throughout the world, between all peoples and nations. Certainly in British inner-city classrooms, and following the horrific watershed of the racist playground murder of Ahmed Ullah at Burnage High School in Manchester in September 1986[9], the words once coined by Fidel Castro have never been more apt: 'The cause of peace and the cause of the working class march side by side.' In the learning and teaching context of literacy that is described in the pages that follow, *peace* is certainly the overall theme of the material being considered and developed, and during a period when, as a twelve year old Greek Cypriot expressed it once in an Fast London classroom, it was at its most stretched and fragile:

> Peace is trembling
> Like a tooth just about to pop.
> Peace should always be with us.

I am referring to December 1990, and the critical period leading up to the expiring of the United Nations deadline ordering the Iraqi troops of President Saddam Hussein to withdraw from Kuwait, which had been invaded the previous August and later annexed. There had been a continuous hectoring by both sides throughout this confrontation, as U.S. troops and their commanders, supported enthusiastically by those of Britain and less so by other nations, had assembled in Saudi Arabia to the south of Kuwait and in a stand-off with the Iraqi armies, had built up their 'Operation Desert Shield' in readiness to attack the Iraqis if they did not withdraw from Kuwait. With the day-to-day stoking up of war-fever by the British tabloid press and Tory and Labour politicians, the moral and religious 'all clear' to begin the conflict being granted by church leaders, and the war-mongering and buffoonery of U.S. President George Bush and Secretary of State James Baker using the fig-leaf of U.N. resolutions against Iraq but with their minds fixed on Kuwaiti oil and preserving the client leadership of the expelled Sabah Kuwaiti ruling dynasty—the chances of a peaceful solution to the Gulf conflict were fast receding, as from the other side came the strident and uncompromising vows that 'Americans would swim in their own blood' if there were war.

From Sheffield to Palestine

This was the broader world context of the work which follows. The much more local context was of a group of thirteen year old school students from various communities studying in a Sheffield comprehensive school and working to improve their command of English literacy by focusing on the key to lasting and genuine peace in the Middle East—the resolution to the question of Palestine, and in particular to the Israeli occupation of the territories of the West Bank. This at a time when anti-Arab racism in Britain was at its most virulent for many years, due much to the tabloid reaction to the depredations in Kuwait provoked by Saddam Hussein's armies. Newspapers like Rupert Murdoch's *Sun* have a long and shameful history of attacking Arabs and Muslims generally, sparked by their hatred of such leaders as Gaddafi or Khomeini in the Middle East—and Muslims struggling against the effects of racism in Britain.[10] Certainly this tabloid 'hype' was contributing to anti-Arab feeling in Sheffield, and being directed towards the local community of Yemenis, many of whose children attended the school. During this same period Yemenis living in the neighbourhood of the school had felt this increased level of racism, and their community centre close to the school had been daubed with racist slogans.

Thus a combination of the enemies of peace near and far: the threat of armed conflict, hostile propaganda and attacks by a reactionary media, racism and ignorance—all contributed to the setting for the classroom work on Palestine. The significant Arab presence in the school (there were students from Syrian, Jordanian, Saudi Arabian and Libyan families also attending, plus an Iraqi teacher who was a refugee from the Saddam Hussein regime) gave this project an additional resonance. The strong Yemeni community association, composed of the families of the Yemeni *arrivants* who had come to work as unskilled labourers in Sheffield's steel industry in the fifties and sixties—held its Arabic language school three evenings a week in the school buildings, and organised a community literacy campaign (in both Arabic and English) in a base in a nearby primary school. The students in the classes concerned were a cross-section of students from the local Yemeni, Pakistani, Somali and white communities. So at least four languages were at work, including the Sheffield variety of English. The school itself was involved in preparations to create a link with, a secondary school in the city of Ramallah on the West Bank as a part of its commitment to internationalism, and the Sheffield students were being encouraged to write letters in both English and Arabic to school students there, in order to consolidate some of this exchange work and get to know the Palestinian students as 'pen-pals'.

The project began by a study of Palestine's recent history, the creation of the state of Israel, the wars against Israel's Arab neighbours and the 1967 occupation of the West Bank. The television film *Children of Fire*[11], telling of experiences of the young people of the West Bank city of Nablus in their *intifada* against the Israeli occupation, was shown, and made a deep impression—particularly upon the Arabic-speaking students, who needed no recourse to subtitles. Discussions on the content of this film were followed up by reading a series of poems about Palestine mostly by Palestinian writers. There was also *Lullaby to a Palestinian Child* (translated from the Urdu) by the outstanding Pakistani poet Faiz Ahmad Faiz, which had a very strong impact especially as so many of the students were of Pakistani origin. Poems by Mahmoud Darwish[12], such as *Identity Card, Victim Number 18, Weddings* and *The First Date* communicated with a simple power the thoughts and feelings of the Palestinian people, as did some of the short and pithy poems of another Palestinian, Samih al-Qasim[13]. As we had the poems in their original Arabic available, we were able to have bilingual readings in the classroom—first the poems in Arabic, read out loud by one of the Arabic speakers, followed by the English translation.

The Linking Imagination

The first response of the students was to the Faiz poem. A Pakistani girl, Sufurah, wrote as if she were a child responding to the soothing lullaby of her mother, but with words of indignation and struggle:

> **Child of palestine**
> Please don't cry Mum,
> When I grow up I'll fight the soldiers with a gun.
> They can break my flesh and bones
> But the only weapons I have are stones.
> With my friends and families too
> I will fight those soldiers for you.
> Don't cry Mum,
> I always dreamed I could play out without fear,
> But every time I do, the soldiers appear.
> When I grip those stones
> I feel that I could break their bones.
> Don't cry Mum,
> When I grow up, one day,
> I'll make those soldiers regret and pay.
> They have closed our schools and relationships.
> Don't cry Mum,
> Now I am part of the *Intifada* mum.
> Don't cry mum,

I had a dream that we defeated the soldiers
And had our country back with us in peace.
Don't cry Mum.

Sufurah Bibi

Another young Pakistani poet, Faheem, composed his couplets in a determined appeal for peace and justice:

Intifada
Why does it have to be this way,
Bullying at night and fighting all day?
I throw stones and rocks with my own bare hands,
Remembering my brother who lay dead in the sands.
Shot by the army and the police -
We don't want a war, we want peace!
Why does it have to be like this,
Losing your family without a bless or a kiss?
I'm losing a part of my life everyday,
Why can't we just throw war away?
I walk the streets in fear of a soldier,
My fist clenched, and within it a boulder.
We all fight as one under the sun,
Yet this war has not been won.
We throw stones, they pull the trigger,
What falls to the ground is a tall, dark figure.
'Ayman Jamous: Ayman Jamous!'
Why can't we call this war to a truce?

Faheem Khan

There was no doubt that the film *Children of Fire* had strongly moved the students. The footage and vivid images of the Palestinian children stoning the Israeli soldiers, the long hours of the curfew, the death of the young *shebab* Ayman Jamous and the Israelis' refusal to allow his body to be released after his killing, the day-by-day disruption to the schooling of Palestinian children—all prompted the viewers to raise these issues in their letters to the students of Ramallah, as if they were asking for confirmation in words of what they had seen so starkly on the screen:

> ... I was very sad because I saw soldiers beat up very small children, and kill some children. I felt very sad when I heard about a young boy who got killed called Ayman Jamous and the soldiers would not hand his body to his family, and they only allowed ten people to come and bury him at night.
> And when I saw those little children throwing stones at those big soldiers who have got guns, my heart felt for them and those little babies who have

got shot and killed. How do those soldiers do it, breaking into schools and homes and slapping children and closing the schools down? How do they do it? I wonder how it feels being there with all those soldiers around you and you can't do anything about it? This has never happened in England.

Or again, from another Pakistani girl:

At school we watched a programme about the sort of life a Palestinian child leads. It differs very much from ours. Ours is very simple whereas yours is to fight for your rights. In the programme very young children were fighting the soldiers back with stones. They promised themselves they would win. After the programme I had knowledge about your lives, how you risk them. What with the soldiers carrying guns and all you have is stones. It was very painful for us to watch that programme. I know that we children in Britain would not have the same courage that you carry in your hearts.

The communal dialogue was extending beyond the classroom, beyond the nations now between Sheffield and Ramallah, but through the pain and resistance of the children of Nablus, as the young people asked their questions and sought authentic answers from only those who know across the world.

Other poems were now emerging about the Intifada, as young Sheffielders took on, through their living imaginations, the struggle of the young Palestinians:

A child of palestine
No school today
No school tomorrow,
Soldiers closed it down.
We fight today
We fight tomorrow,
Then sleep a sleepless night.

Life is a nightmare
That the Intifada is trying to change.
Maybe soon
Maybe too late
Maybe today
Or maybe tomorrow -
Soon, we hope and pray.

Stones in hand
Ready to throw,
Maybe now
And forever more!

Dreams of the future
In our minds.
Peace will never come to soon,
We've waited long enough.

Why don't they go?
And leave us alone.
Give us back our land
And leave us in peace -
Because we'll never leave,
Here we'll stay.

Tricks and games
They play,
Leave us bombs
Wrapped like chocolate
For little children killed this way.

We children are
Beaten and hit
By soldiers that should be far away.
Our homes are wrecked
And yet we have to stay inside.
Curfew times we have -
They're not worthy to live and laugh.

Soon we hope that peace will come,
I hope that war's not just begun:

We play games
As we live,
Play-fight
Then fight for real,
No weapons but stones.

Even babies
Are shot and killed,
Families grow very close.

We wish
For peace and tranquillity,
We've lived like this
For too long.

Yet we'll never give up without a fight!
We have the right!

Marie Howe

Children of Palestine
My life is a war.
During the day I'm a *shebab*
Fighting for my rights.
Kids from five out in the streets
Throwing stones, lighting fires from tyres.
The children run when they see a soldier.
Some days there's a curfew -
Being trapped in your own house, all through the day
And all through the night.
When I go to sleep at night
I wish it would all end when the morning's bright.
Soldiers close the school,
Take the kids and beat them.
The *Intifada* is my fight.

Sajid Mustafa

A child of palestine
Fighting for my rights,
Risking my life.
Me and my friends playing with stones,
Then going out and fighting with stones.
Small or big it's just the same
Get caught by the soldiers, get beaten or shot,
Lighting fires on the streets so the soldiers wouldn't get us.
Close the school, take the children and beat them,
Make you stay home all day and night in the curfew.
But we will still make our flag stay in the air!

Mumtaz Ali

Intifada
As the last stones of freedom slip through my fingers, hate
and anger run through my body.
Why doesn't my country belong to me? Why do I feel like
a prisoner in my own home?
Our family were never so close, but the fighting has brought
us closer. We all seem to be one, fighting for the same
thing.
My brother and I used to fight side by side in the streets,
until one day there was a loud noise

And my brother fell to the ground just like a ripe apple
would.
My brother to me will always be a hero, a martyr who died
for his beliefs.
I just hope it ends soon, so my brother's soul can rest like
the others.
And Palestine can be one once again.

Corin Ovendale

And a Somali boy looked beyond Israel towards the weapon suppliers and profiteers
of Israeli repression beyond the Atlantic:

Intifada

Life in Palestine is unbearable. I call it Palestine because it's my country,
not theirs. It's a Muslim country, not a Jewish country. In our school it's another
day, another death. They come and kill. Why, I ask myself, why oh Allah, do
they kill us and beat us up? Our playground, it is pure blood red. Boys and
girls with their brains beaten out. We do not believe in guns or bombs or
making them die. We just want them to leave us, our families, our friends,
our houses and our homeland.

We throw stones, they pull the trigger. What is their hobby, murder? Or is
it the enjoyment of seeing us suffer with pain and sorrow? When we throw,
they get grazed. When they shoot, we die. How can they sleep, knowing
they've killed someone's loved one? Old women, men, children and babies?
They will not rest until they've wiped us out. In the West people have freedom
and love, but the Israelis do not know the word love, nor loyalty. All they
know is murder and violence.

Every night for two years I wept for my family who were killed for swearing
at the soldiers. I was out shopping and when I came back I saw the blood of
my family. I want my Mum to wipe my eyes and cuddle me, and my father to
pick me up and swing me, my brother to play games with me like football
and my only sister to love me like her baby. But alas, they've gone now. I live
in the mountains at night and throw stones in the light. One day we shall live
as people and not as hostages in our homes.

For every Palestinian that dies, the days get closer when we will rule our
country. Until that time we wait until Allah gives us our birthright back, and
then we won't shoot the Israelis. We'll let their consciences sort out what's
wrong or right. America can help us by stopping their supply of weapons. But
to them, money is more precious than life.

Musa Ibrahim

These responses were in their own way, through the power of their imaginative
empathy, re-creating Palestine in the minds of the students. This process of imaginative

fire, entering the lives of others, was expressed very nakedly by one of the Pakistani girls, who wrote, 'Don't just think about yourself, think about other people in the world. They may be in the war, while we are in England.' The same point was made by another girl writing about the young people of South Africa, struggling in the townships against the effects of apartheid

Immortal
They'll live forever,
And never die.
They're joined to us,
More than ever.
We breathe for them.
Fight for them,
Live for them.
We are them.

Sallie Higgins

Now it was Palestine and Sajid, another Pakistani boy, directly provoked by the lyrics of Mahmoud Darwish, imagined himself as the lover of a Palestinian patriot who leaves to carry on a struggle from exile:

Love in Palestine
Now you go to fight,
How do I know if you will return?
You have gone now,
The time has passed and you're not back.
Oh my love, your children cry!
I hope you will be here to see them live.
For a year now I have been waiting
For you to walk through that door!

Sajid Mustafa

And Leanne, after reading some testimonies describing the daily routine of patrolling Israeli soldiers who were ordered to harass Palestinian school students, disrupt their classes and close their schools, decided to set down her version of such a soldier's experiences, and the shame and tension racking his mind:

The side of the soldiers
A Palestinian child started throwing stones at me. Some of them come very close to hitting me. It hurts me deep down inside to see that all the children hate me. I can understand why the adults hate me but why does it have to be a child? Some of them are only three to five years of age. It gives me pain to see the children hating me so much and them being so young. I know I

shouldn't, but I keep a diary of what happens day by day. If anyone finds out, I would be punished and the diary would be destroyed.

These are some of the days in the diary, some of the worst days, that is.

Monday 15th November

Today we made a scene in the school and all the kids stopped what they were doing and looked at me with anger and hatred in their faces. The teacher was stood there looking very timid, frightened and frozen stiff with fear. The children started throwing paper at us. A piece of paper hit one of the soldiers and it made him mad. He walked very boldly up to the child and started hitting him. He hit the boy across the face with the end of his gun. Blood gashed from the boy's face. The soldier then kicked him and threw him against a wall. There was blood everywhere.

Only three of us went into that school and yet we caused so much pain towards that child. Silence broke, and we left, feeling guilt and rage inside us.

Friday 19th November

Today we walked the streets angry. A woman was trying to hurry up and get inside her house. She was pregnant. She was scared of losing her baby, you could tell by the look on her face. It said fear all over.

She swore at us, so one of the soldiers came up to her and kicked her in the stomach. She swore at us again and fell to the ground with pain. I turned away in disgust. I went up to her and with pain inside me, hit her across the face with the end of my gun. He took her away with us. All the people came out of their doors, screaming for her. I also felt their pain.

Some of the soldiers started trying to kiss her. She turned away, so they shot her for her rejection. I just stood there watching.

Nearly every day was like this. Either someone got hurt, or they were killed by us. I am not proud of what I have done but it is too late now because I am a part of the hate and pain. I am now destroying my diary in fear of someone finding it.

Leanne Cater

Among the many poems, letters and prose passages coming directly from these students' engagement with Palestine and its people's striving for peace-with-justice was this, poem, which in the week after it was written, was read out loud by its writer to the assembled parents, students and school governors at the school's Presentation Evening. The poem followed closely upon the events of October 1990, when 21 young Palestinians were killed by Israeli soldiers in Jerusalem, as they demonstrated to defend the Temple Mount mosque. A national black newspaper[16] had published a harrowing photograph in the aftermath of these events, depicting the father of one of the victims praying on the flagstones at the exact place where his son had been shot down. Nadia, a Yemeni girl, tried to express with her poem the terrible grief of this father, the loss and denials that were deep in his mind—and which in the final line turn into his stolen country itself.

My son
My son
Who I loved dearly,
Who protected the Holy House

My son,
Of all the sons in the world,
Who got shot and killed
And who loved his family

My son
Who I protected all my life
Brought up ..
And bred,
Who I lived my life for.
Now I don't care
Whether I live or die.

My son,
I pray on your blood,
Hoping you would come back -
Why couldn't it be me instead?
I'll do anything to get you back!

When I saw him
Lying there
On the stones,
Helpless and cold
I did not want to believe it.
He was dead.

When my son fell down dead on the stones
I felt I could weep forever!
So everyone in the world could hear me.
People asked 'Why, why do you weep?'
I told them if you take a knife
And cut part of yourself -
You would feel pain and cry.
That's why I weep -
Because I feel the pain!

The saddest thing is, he was so young,
Like a flower
Just bloomed within Spring
And suddenly, just died
In front of my eyes!
I felt the life just slip from my body,
And this pain is shared—
With every Palestinian—
Young and old!

My son
What have you done to deserve this?
I was just looking forward
To carry your first-born!

My son,
It was not so long ago
That I held you in my arms with joy and pride—
The first moment you were born.

Now my son
I hold you
Dead in my arms,
My heart filled with sorrow,
My eyes filled with tears
And all this for you, my Palestine!

                                              Nadia Saleh

Literacy, the Imagination and Peace

The twin hopes of peace and justice were never far from these children's words. Yet all around them in the newspapers their parents read, the television screens that dominated their living rooms, the sounds from their radios—were reports and images of the relentless training, and manoeuvres of the thousands of troops, tanks, aircraft and warships being primed in Saudi Arabia and readied for attack. Prophecies of chemical biological and nuclear warfare, together with the endless burning of oilfields and environmental disasters were being declared day after day. Even one of their own schoolmates, a local boy with a Saudi Arabian father who had been on an extended visit to his family in the Gulf, had been called up for military service by the Saudi army, and the school was writing letters to the authorities of that country, petitioning for him to be released go he could be released, return to England and continue his studies at the school. Sick, warmongering humour was the order of the day, with so-called comedians like Jim Davidson—the favourite 'comic' of the British Armed

Forces—whose answer to his own question 'what, have Baghdad and Hiroshima got in common?' was 'Nothing—yet!'[17] To be building up their own language, together—with such a growing understanding of the injustices behind the tension and violence in a critical region of the world, and using their imaginations to reach into the consciousness of those truly involved, to achieve that understanding—all this was not easy in the heart of such unpromising and bellicose surroundings.

Yet such work, a part of a curriculum of extended literacy for young people that fuses the abilities to develop new skills with words, to sharpen human consciousness and stretch the imagination to enter the lives of others in a shared world, creating new, communal forms of expression—becomes more and more essential in our schools, even as the stranglehold of the state's 'National Curriculum' seeks to squeeze out such human solidarity and breadth of understanding. Certainly the young Sheffield students recognized very quickly the bond that the Palestinian people felt with their own country—their 'life-land', as one girl expressed it. Their understanding had already travelled a long distance.

Notes

1 See Freire, Paulo, *The Pedagogy of the Oppressed*, Penguin, 1972, London; *Education: the Practice of Freedom* , Writers and Readers 1974, London; *Pedagogy in Process* , 1978, Writers and Readers, London; and *Literacy: Reading the Word and the World* , 1987, Routledge and Kegan Paul, London.

2 See Hirshon, Sheryl, *And Also teach them to Read* , 1983, Lawrence Hill and Co., Connecticut and Lanshear, Colin with Lawler, Moira, *Literacy, Schooling, and Revolution* , 1987, Falmer Press, Lewis; for excellent accounts of the literacy campaign in Nicaragua; Searle, Chris, *A Blindfold Removed, Ethiopia's Struggle for Literacy* , 199, Karia, London describes the literacy campaign in Ethiopia.

3 Searle, Chris, Classrooms of Resistance, 1975, Writers and Readers, London; also *The World in a Classroom* , 1977, Writers and Readers, London.

4 For an account of the literacy campaign in Grenada see Searle, Chris, *Words Unchained: Language and Revolution in Grenada*, 1984, Zed Press, London. For descriptions of literacy processes in Mexico and Bolivia read Archer, David and Costello, Patrick, *Literacy and Power: The Latin American Battleground* , 1990, Earthscan, London.

5 See *A Blindfold Removed*, op cit.

6 See *Children and their Primary Schoolst a Report of the Central Advisory Council for Education*, 1967, Volume 1, Part 2: The Growth of the Child, London.

7 See Searle, Chris, 'A Common Language' in *Race and Class*, Autumn 1983, Volume XXV, Institute of Race Relations, London.

8 See Searle, Chris, 'From Forster to Baker: the New Victorianism and the Struggle for Eduoation' in *Race and Class*, April-June 1989, Volume XXXI Institute of Race Relations, London.

9 See *Murder in the Playground*, The Report of the Macdonald Inquiry into racism and racial violence in Manchester schools, 1989, Longsight Press, London.

10 See Searle, Chris, *Your Daily Dose: Racism and 'The Sun'*, 1989, Campaign for Press and Broadcasting Freedom, London.

11 *Children of Fire*, a film by Mai Masri, 1990, MTC Productions, London.

12 See Darwish, Mahmoud, *The Music of Human Flesh*, 1980, Heinemann, London, and *Victims of a Map*, 1984, Al Saqi,London.

13 See *Victims of a Map*, op cit.

14 See *Freedom Children: a tribute in poetry to the young people of South Africa from the young people of Sheffield*, 1990, Sheffield City Council, Sheffield

15 See Israeli soldiers' accounts in Aronson, Geoffrey, Israel, *Palestinians and the Intifada*, 1990, Kegan Paul International, London.

16 *Caribbean Times*, 27 October 1990, London

17 *Morning Star*, 4 January 1991, London

'OTHERS IN MYSELF, MYSELF IN OTHERS': THE IMAGINATION AND INTERNATIONALISM (1993)

Perhaps there has never been a time such as now when so much sheer individualism spreads itself across our education system. During the Thatcher years, the leader herself frequently proclaimed that there was no such thing as a community. This concept has now developed into an institutionalised selfishness, wherein her mind-forms take concrete expression through the effects of the Education Acts her ministers established. Schools are all but cut off from the protection of the local education authority, their commission is to fight it out with each other for pupil heads and an increased budget share. They are to contest for the right to survive—closure becomes a constant threat if they become too small, too 'unviable' in 'delivering' the National Curriculum or hold too many 'surplus places'. Like these phantom units, the schools themselves are permanently faced by being 'taken out', particularly if they are in hard-pressed inner-city areas and their students are working class and black. They must become the sacrifice for a greater budgetary allocation to the well-resourced, larger and thriving, schools in the middle class suburbs.

As the National Curriculum grips the classroom ethos, in its imposed parameters, convergent and narrow perspectives on knowledge, its assessment procedures barred up by regular testing and terminal examinations, we see one constant image: the walls are being re-erected. We shall see less of students cooperating, working together, discovering solidarity through learning. We see the individual child as we knew ourselves at school, with a pen in one hand and the other hand and an arm making a wall around her study, bending over her work, preventing it from being seen by her classmates 'This is mine: Sir ... she's looking over my work!'

In institutional terms, this restored educational culture of walls found its true expression a few weeks ago in Sheffield, when a secondary headteacher, complaining to the local press about the insufficiency of her school budget, called for smaller schools in the city to be closed so her school could take more money—specifically to pay for a local security firm to make a nightly patrol around the school's buildings.[1]

In this context as young minds face the threat of being programmed as discrete and detached conciousnesses, seeing knowledge as single atoms in the classroom, the unifying and challenging power of the imagination takes on an even greater importance. In the words of Sivanandan, it is 'to see others in myself and myself in others, which is love; to understand what is owed to them and what is owed to me, which is justice; to become them, which is imagination'.[2]

Individualism turns the imagination upon itself, twisting and distorting its syncretic power, its impulse towards human solidarity. In progressive times when struggling humans look out from themselves for union and collective strength, the imagination comes to demonstrate its true power. In such times "people learn what they might have been and discover what belongs to them apart from their single lives.'[3] For imagination brings empathy, allows humans to become other humans, take on their consciousness and change their own as a result. In that sense they never leave the other. That 'momentary holding' seized by the imagination—as described by John Berger—realises a new unity and brings humans and their lives and achievements together as one. Here, as the Bengali Tagore would have dared to describe it, 'the crowd of worlds rush in, greeting each other.'[4]

This is what Paul Robeson did with his voice, what Neruda, Hikmet, Faiz, Neto and Darwish achieved with their poetry what Carpentier, El Saadawi, Ngugi, Mulk Raj Anand, Ousmane, Toni Morrison and Lamming show in their novels, what Victor Jara, Ewan MacColl and Woody Guthrie speak through their lyrics, what Shakespeare, Brecht and Lorca moulded in their drama. Through the impact of all their living words people can learn of what we yet might be in these last years of our century, and how we can make a daily meeting place for progress.

In such a place we not only meet these giants of word and image: we meet among ourselves and find each other, millions of us young and old across the world. For we find excellence and community in the ordinary, in people like us as we share each other's lives and struggles. Such a place was revolutionary Africa in the mid-seventies and one of its liberated areas was the new independent nation of Mozambique. Here was a country finding itself, a people determined to free themselves after centuries of humiliation and colonial oppression—with its comrade nations like Tanzania, Angola and Guinea-Bissau. As a fifty year old nurse wrote in his night class as he discovered the English language:

> ... their suffering became life's steps,
> their human life was forgotten—
> the only way to live was to bend down.
> Our country was separated
> from the whole world,
> its life was a tiny thing.
> But today we have solidarity and brotherhood
> And Mozambique is our light and guide.

This was Africa proudly taking a leading place in progress, its people full of pride, purpose and imagination. A school student wrote

> Africa
> Exploited and oppressed

Today rises and says,
'Freedom, workers of the world!'

and his classmate set down that

Our freedom isn't complete
While there are oppressed people.

His empathy reached out towards

... Chile and Namibia in imperialism's cage,
blood irritates the prisons,
in bantustans in South Africa.

In now times in Europe and America it becomes more and more important to remember words and thoughts such as these, for they show the routes that the new Mozambicans took to change their lives and the mentality that guided them. These words were allied to work, organisation and struggle. As their President, Samora Machel, found his own words to describe their progress:

The complexes which are manifested express the weight of the old mentality we still carry inside us. The struggle for us to destroy this legacy is one of the essential moments of creation of the new mentality.[5]

Essential moments, those forged by the imagination, like those taken to create an image, a sentence—or for a school student, to make a poem which leaps from the past to the presents

The Worker Yesterday
Dawn ...
The worker thinks
thinks of the whip.

Dawn ...
The worker thinks
thinks of the dust in the mines.

Dawn ...
The worker thinks
thinks he is capable.

Dawn ...
Now the worker
thinks of the communal tasks.

Jose Maria de Carlos

Yet who was to foretell in those ebullient days of building and transforming and open solidarity with the Zimbabwean people fighting Ian Smith's racist rule, what would follow for Mozambique? Who could see the terrorising and division of a brave people, the intervention of the murderous power to the south, the bankrolling and arming of bandits and carnage-mongers, the killing of an inspirational leader, the organized famine and massacres, the attack on hope and achievement. Perhaps in the 1977 words of this sixteen year old student, Joaquim Vilanculos, there is prophecy as well as empathy:

The Worker fights for Freedom
I arise
I look through the window of my bedroom
And I say
It's time ...
The clarity of the growing day
is the end of my joy!
Because I know to whom the day belongs.
More than a drop of my blood will be sucked,
Because I know who profits from my work -
And my money, paid in taxes
Will be used to buy more guns, more grenades
To assassinate my people
To oppress my people
To stop me dead when I say I'm exploited,
To force me to pay more taxes.
... ahhhhh
I'm a peasant
From the rising to the setting of the sun
In the black dust of the exploited earth,
I'm a worker
I'm a fighter for freedom
I'm a poor worker.

Such thoughts and fears have been set free by the imagination reaching outward—a power extended by contemporary Mozambican writers like Mia Couto and Lina Magaia, who are helping to carry their nation forward through its present agony.[6] In their words too, like those of the young Mozambicans of 1977, there is the breaking of walls and the opening of doors, for

people have blood, tears
and great distress.
People have the great keys

to open the doors
of freedom.

We need these 'great keys' now. Despite 'Standard Assessment Tasks', 'Key Stages' and all the paraphernalia of National Curriculum orders, what they can unlock for us now is precious and essential. Two fourteen year old Pakistan girls reflect upon Africa too in 1991, using those same keys in Sheffield, England. On June 16 they remembered, and put down their own words for the youth in Soweto in 1976.

In detention
I'm in detention
For not doing my homework.

They're in detention
For crying for freedom.

I'll be home in two hours
They'll be home in two months
Or maybe more.

They might not even come back.
They'll be tortured,
I won't.
They'll be hanged like clothing
I won't.

How many lives
Will be lost?
Mow many mothers will shed tears?
How many loved ones will die,
Die before, Africa gets Its freedom?

Naeeda Razzak

Hector's story
As he marched,
freedom on his lips,
Hands in air,
Screaming, shouting,
"Africa Is mine!"
Suddenly,
Soldiers shout,
You felt, I ran,
You bled, I cry,
You died, I lived,
My son, a martyr.

Shameem Rasaq

Fifteen years before this, in a classroom in Nampula, a city in the north of Mozambique, a group of African students had written this collective poem, just one year after the resistance and massacre that was to become such a huge turning point of the struggle of the South African people.

Soweto.
Your streets are great rivers of blood
Pregnant with corpses.
Soweto:
The cries of children
Calling to the power of the people
That neither the hostile faces of the guards
Nor the guns managed to smother,
This great desire
This flame of freedom.

The united hands
Of this great people
Firmly clenched
Shall lay in ruins the foundations of apartheid.

It is more than saluting
The voice of reason

It is more than seeing
The reason for the struggle

It is more than being certain
Of the awaited victory

We are with you—one entire people
Of the one Africa
Who arise from the long night
To destroy the chains of oppression -
We are with you!

Within these last three poems the imagination, reason and their power to make union through time and continents, have broken down the walls erected between separate perspectives of curriculum and knowledge. In 1991, while President George Bush urged the Kurdish people to rise up against Saddam Hussein and allowed them to be his sacrifice—and British Prime Minister John Major squeaked about 'safe havens', students in Sheffield sought to imagine and understand the conditions of the Kurdish agony and struggle.

Under the black blanket

We Kurds are under the black blanket
And the rest of the countries are under the blue.
We dream of a country of our own,
A dream which someday will come true.
An Iraqi once said that I shouldn't dream,
It isn't good for me, and it's hard to be true.
I said to him, 'a dream doesn't hurt'
He said, 'it will hurt If it doesn't come true'.
Why are we under black blanket
And not under the blue?
Why is it so hard for us to dream?

Nahid Aziz

The Kurdish People: Halabja

I was at my friend's house when it happened. We saw people lying on street, people shouting and then falling. I tried to run, to shut myself and my friend away in a room, but all I could think of were people dying and the terrible screams of anguish that could be heard all around us.

My friend's voice broke through my thoughts and we ran. We knocked on doors and shouted through windows to let the people know what was happening.

We were very lucky that the gas had not reached us yet. We held handkerchiefs and bits of torn cloth to our faces. It helped but not much.

As we ran people all round us were falling at our feet.

Then I realised that my family were in danger also. When we reached my house I could see my brother standing over the dead body of my sister. My parents where nowhere in sight. As we ran from room to room I began to get more worried. I still couldn't find them. When my brother joined in the search, I could tell he had been crying but he didn't say anything.

We found them at last hidden under bed. They had closed all the windows and doors when they found my sister lying on the floor. The rest of the family was safe but my friend's family was another matter.

That was three years ago and to this day I can remember seeing all those people lying In the streets.

Since then some terrible things have happened but none as bad as that.

We are trying to pick up the pieces and start again but we have no country and we feel we have no friends but the mountains that help to hide us.

Marie Howe

Empathy needs to come much closer to home too. In 1992 the British government was pressing to pass through parliament its Asylum Bill which threatened to curtail the rights of asylum in Britain for refugees fleeing from tyranny and death. During this times, schools in many British cities were welcoming the children of refugee families, many of whom had endured horrific experiences. Families from northern Somalia, in particular from the bombarded cities of Hargeisa and Burao, arrived in Sheffield. As they and their parents told their stories of escape from the soldiers of Siad Barré's tribalistic and brutal government, their new classmates strove to imagine what the last few months of life had been like for them. In the following two pieces, a Pakistani and white English girl reconstruct their struggle. We invited into their class some members of the local Somali Community Association to hear the students read these words. As they listened, the recognition was intense and they openly wept as Safina and Vicki read of the months and moments they had known themselves.

My great escape

'Solomon wake up, wake up! we have to leave now!' My mother said.

I woke to the sounds of bullets being fired, screams from children and wails from grieving mothers, who were soon also shot. I sat up, stirred by the terrible sounds. My mother grabbed me and threw my baby brother into my arms. She then ran and helped my father collect some belongings and rounded the rest of the family together. There were sounds of trucks coming, more shooting went on and I could hear people screaming and shouting. What was going on out there? Confused and frightened I clung onto my mother, holding her tight while we made our escape.

My poor mother had my two sisters hanging off one leg, and me on the other.

Then she had a box full of supplies and utensils and my baby brother in her other arm. Meanwhile my father bad a bundle of clothes on his back and two boxes, full to the top, of utensils.

We lived in Hargeisa, in northern Somalia. It was such a lovely place until civil war occurred. I used to go to school with all my friends. We had books and pencils but now we have got nothing, not even a school. Our school was bombarded for no reason all. 'Hurry up Solomon, you're dragging behind," my mother said. I quickly caught up to my mother and clung onto her leg.

We walked on and on, through dry deserts sharp rocks. My feet got caught on the rocks and bled and were very sore. One of my sisters had collapsed with malnutrition, for we were running out of food. My mother looked ill, but she still carried on walking with a strong expression on her face. I tried to imagine what she was thinking by staring hard at her and concentrating. It seemed to me that my mother was thinking nice things like that we will be *together* soon, and *happy*. These two words were her goals which she had to achieve. This is why she carried on walking so strongly, but yet she was so ill. My father looked very limp and ill. The expression on his face was a defeated and weak look, and he was going to give up. He still carried on walking though, looking over his shoulder cautiously from time to time.

Nomads would also approach us and offer us food. We gladly accepted and ate heartily. We would also take that as an advantage to rest a little for we hardly ever slept.

Four weeks had passed. My little sister had died. She died of starvation and exhaustion. We couldn't even bury her, we just left her under some bushes. I wouldn't leave her, I couldn't, how could I? She lay there so peacefully and unharmed. As I kissed her forehead a teardrop fell onto her cheek. I wiped it away with my hand. Her skin was still soft but stone cold. I ran on towards my mother and hugged her. I was scared and yet angry.

"Is that what happens to you when you die?' I asked. "Yes,' my mother answered.

"Then what happens?" I said.

"You're too young too understand," my father said. He sounded angry and upset. I could share this anger with him, for I could feel the same way he felt. Who do these people think they were? Killing innocent people. Shooting them, or starving them. My sister had died because of this war and there was no justice.

Another week passed, we met up with another group of Somalis. We heard we were getting closer to the border, and that we would be in Ethiopia quite soon.

There we would probably meet up with some relatives and be happy again. I skipped merrily as I thought this thought. I soon suddenly stopped and turned around. I heard gunshots, "Mother! Father!" I shouted but nobody answered. People started to run shouting, 'The Government soldiers are here."

I turned back around and started to run, when my father called me back in a weak voice. He was shot in both legs and was unable to move. Besides him lay my dead mother and little sister.

My father passed me my baby brother and told me to go and run on. "No!" I shouted, I couldn't leave my father to be killed. 'I will not leave without you!," I said and tried dragging him with me. It was hopeless.

"Go!" my father shouted "Be brave! run fast or you'll be shot too!". 'I can't,' I shouted. The government soldiers were now gaining and so I turned round to run, my eyes welling with tears. I couldn't leave my father there so helpless. I ran and ran. I kept thinking of the thought my mother thought and ran on. More gunshots went off and I screamed for I realised that my father was probably killed.

Night fell, but I still carried on running. The Government soldiers had gained quite a lot now. I was very tired, hungry, sad but most of all, lonely except for my baby brother who couldn't speak. All my life I had stayed with my parents. Now I have none. No one to credit me, no one love me and no one to hug me. I was there alone in the world, with a little brother to took after.

I soon reached Ethiopia and into the Ethiopian camps. The camps were in
Horshin. Me and my brother needed serious attention and so we were kept at
another camp, where I met my uncle. My uncle come from Sheffield in England
and was a doctor. Once be had heard about the bad news of the civil war, he
came to help. My uncle used to write to me a lot back home, even though I
couldn't read. He used to send me clothes and photographs of him and his
family (That's how I recognised him). Once we were better we were to go to
Sheffield with my uncle to live with his family.

Safina Rashid

Escape From War

As I am walking along the long stretch of desert,
I am wondering if we will ever be free.
Free from bribes
and especially, free from war.

A I look back
I see my city of War that I am trying to escape from
the city is Hargeisa,

As I look in front, all I see is sand
and more importantly.
people in pain.
The old people struggling behind,
The pregnant women wanting to give birth quickly—
Most of them already have.

We have no water and no food,
except occasionally,
When the nomads bring us bits.

Our feet are also in pain
Because every now and again
we come to hard-surfaced roads,
And all we have are soft and flimsy sandals
Which are barely there.

We have to pass through blocks on these roads,
the soldiers press us for bribes as we pass
And I arm watching the people with no money getting
punished.

With all this happening around me
I am wondering If I will ever be free.

Vicki Robertson

The 1931 Gulf War brought to the surface much underlying racism within British society and the British people. Stoked up by the tabloid press, led by Murdoch's inglorious *Sun*, all Asians became Iraqis and all Muslims became Saddam's supporters. British Pakistanis, Indians, Bangladeshis, Sri Lankans and Yemenis all became the targets for racist abuse and attack throughout Britain's inner-cities. The following poetry and prose pieces were written when fear still gripped British Asian communities particularly their women, many of whom had faced the direct fire of racist hostility. Asma, from a Bangladeshi family, genuinely caught the force of media assault as well as physical attack in her story. The same indignation at ignorance and brutality courses through the words of the Pakistani girl's, Shameem and Nahda. Finally, Elizabeth's account shows the depth of an English girls understanding and her creative strength wrought through 'the energy of love'[8]—which John Berger identifies as the source of the imagination.

The Gulf War at home

It was a cold Monday morning when I was walking down the street—to go to the paper shop. I was thinking what was going to happen today with the Gulf War? How many people are going to lose their lives? How many women will become widows? How many mothers will weep for their ever-gone children? Or how many children will weep for their parents? But that only Allah would know.

I then looked around the rows of terraced houses, most of the curtains were closed. I walked on. Everywhere I looked there were big signs saying "STOP THE WAR IN THE GULF". The last time I looked at the same sign board it said 'GET OUT OF KUWAIT". There were even papers stuck on the bus shelter saying something about war in the Gulf too.

The corner shop which was owned by a Pakistani man was vandalised and windows had been smashed by white youths because of all this. I looked at the shop and shook my head, not knowing what was going to happen next.

I walked on, then entered the paper shop. Already there were two women in the shop, they just stared at me as if I was just something out of space. The woman behind the counter I had known for many years, would smile at me or say something to me any time I come into the shop, but today she gave me a dirty look.

Her son was one of the servicemen In the Gulf War. She started to say, "if Saddam Hussein didn't invade Kuwait my son wouldn't have been there", she said that as loud as she could so I could hear, but to me it seemed all she thought about was her son. After all he did consider joining the Army, and all his mother could do Is take it out on a black customer.

I went where the newspapers were, and on the first newspaper I looked at (which was *The Sun*) it said in big capital letters "BASTARD OF BAGHDAD". These words took most of the page which also had two pictures of the British prisoners of war on it. The way *The Sun* was describing everything it was like Saddam Hussein's the devil and the troops were angels that God had sent to save him from devastating the world.

A fat woman walked in the shop, she lived across the road to us. She worked as a cleaner in one of the schools. She picked up a copy of *The Sun* and paid for it, reading the headline as she went out. A builder come in and bought a copy of *The Sun* too.

I once remember my uncle saying papers like the *Sun* and *The Daily Mirror* were 'toilet paper' and were full of rubbish. I then took a copy of *The Daily Mail*, paid for it and come out.

As I was walking up the road reading the front-page of the paper, I met a man who I knew and called Uncle. He comes to the Asian Community Centre. He said to me if I could help him set the place up for a meeting which was going to the held in the evening. They were going to discuss the problems Asian people are facing here because of the war.

I came home and told mum about it, then I set off for school. I come home from school. It was about 5.00 clock, so I got off to the Community Centre. It wasn't that for from our house, it was just up road from us. As I was going, I was thinking because of this war innocent people have been abused and assaulted by white police for no purpose at all. I remember when I was small teachers and parents would say that 'fighting never solved anything but made things worse", but on the other hand I think, why are they having this war?

I entered the Community Centre, Uncle was there only. He asked me if I could put the leaflets out on the table, which were something about the Gulf War.

Just then, as I was doing that the door slammed open and three white youths appeared. We both started staring at them, and froze for a minute as they helped themselves to everything. Then one of them who had blonde hair and about three earrings said to Uncle, 'do you speak English?' trying to make an Asian accent and moving his hand at the same time, but he didn't amuse anyone. While all this was happening the other two men were making paper aeroplanes with the leaflets about the Gulf War, and were saying they were from the National Front and that they wanted us out from here now.

At that moment I had the feeling that something very unpleasant was going to happen.

At that instant Uncle got up and told them to clear off. The one with blonde hair came closer to him and said, 'who the heck are you to tell us to clear off grandad, this is our land and this crap community stuff is on it'. While we were chatting on, the others were shouting and screaming abusive things towards us.

This time they took It too for. I had to say something to them, so I did, I told them to learn more about the world, and see what white people are doing to our country. He to looked at me and come towards me chewing slowly and said.

'Listen you, if I want your advice I'll ask for it.'

Another of them shouted out that we were all terrorists and we should be sent back to our own country, because if we stay here we might terrorise this country, and that all us Muslims were savages. As he played the entertainer, others started laughing and shouting out 'savages'!".

As this was burning up my soul, it was as If all we blacks were powerless. I told them to get out. The one with blonde hair told me to shut up, and go and cover myself top to bottom in black clothes. This made things even worse. I could feel anger and hate building up inside me towards white people.

I said to the blonde-haired one 'you should be ashamed of yourself for what you said". This made him very angry, so he told me to apologise to him for what I had said, but instead I spat on his face. He quickly lifted his hand up to hit me as hard as he could, but Uncle came and got hold of him. He pushed him to the ground as the others started on him too. I come and started hitting the white boys on their backs knowing there was no use in that because for those moments I was useless.

The blonde-haired one come rushing in, grabbing me by the arm then beating me to the floor, saying to me that be would finish us, like the Western troops will finish Saddam Hussein. I looked to my left. Uncle was there getting up and bleeding. But why, why were they beating a poor old harmless man who was just minding his own business?

I started screaming for help, but no one was there to hear my screams. The boy told me to shut up or he would chop me into four pieces. They were beating us, imagining that we were Saddam Hussein himself. They then heard a noise coming toward the front door, and the white boys ran as fast as they could through the back door.

I couldn't move my feet, I felt like screaming, but who was going to hear my screams? I wanted to cry louder but who was going to lend me their shoulder to cry on? I thought 'why us? What have we done to harm whites, to deserve this punishment?

Then a woman come through the door. She was Uncle's wife, she was shocked when she saw us in that state. She was going to phone the police, but I told her not to because it would make things worse. We both helped Uncle up and washed the blood off his wounds, and went to their house In the car.

When we got there, I cleaned myself up as If nothing had ever happened and Uncle did the some. He agreed that I was right not to tell the police because It would get worse.

His wife brought me home in her car, I couldn't tell my parents what had happened. So she told them. They were very upset and were scared that I thought I couldn't go to school anymore, and that I would be trapped in the house for ever. But at least we felt safer at home, and we were away from white people attacking us because of the Gulf War.

                                                                    Asma Bibi

Dread

I dread the narrow streets,
I dread the screams of racism,
I dread the hatred of white and black,
I dread leaving my home
And stepping into the open.

I dread my child going to school,
I dread him to be seen,
I dread him to be beaten.
I dread him to grow up
In a world of fear.

I dread the Gulf War,
I dread to think how It would end,
I dread to hear the bombs explode,
I dread to think of the lifeless bodies
Floating in a river of blood.

I wish it would end,
If it doesn't I should leave,
Go back to where peace lies,
Surely, this isn't the place for me.

                                                              Shameem Rasaq

Victims

"Today Iraq launched one of its first scud missiles towards Saudi Arabia but fortunately the missile was brought down by an American Patriot Missile."

I got up and switched off the television. The Gulf War affects people thousands of miles away like the black people in this country, because racist attacks have increased because of the Gulf War. My friend and her sister own a shop which was vandalised, the windows were broken but nothing was taken and racist graffiti was painted all over. They are now scared to come out of their homes. I just want to know why these people judge us by the colour of our skins. They don't know what we want, who we supported and the fear inside us because none of us want to be part of an increase in racism.

I went and got my coat. The shopping had to be done. I locked all the doors, I stepped outside the house, the threats still lingering in my mind.

There were not many black people on our street. There was a group of white youths standing further down the street, so I crossed over instinctively when I got near them. As I approached closer they began talking loudly among themselves. I looked to find them staring in my direction. One stood on the edge of the pavement. I glanced at him, he was a tall slim teenager.

'Hey you Paki' he shouted.

I felt sick at his ignorance. These people didn't even know the difference between Pakistani and Arab people.

The others began to giggle and laugh, giving the first one more encouragement. He came across the road and started shouting.

"You Saddam supporters, if you people think you can take on the rest of the world, why don't you come and take me on?" he shouted. 'You black people support that bastard Saddam!"

He pushed me. I was scared, I didn't know what to do. I stepped aside and started walking. Now all of them started shouting things like, 'Go back to Bombay you Paki!'

'We want the West you Paki', shouted another.

When I was clear away I was scared, so I went to the telephone booth and phoned my brother at college. When he came to the phone I told him what had happened. He said he would pick me up and take me shopping and drop me home. I waited for a couple of minutes. I was a little shaky. I was wondering that the white youths didn't know much. They were calling me a Paki and telling me to go back to Bombay. Well I'm a Pakistani and come from Pakistan. Not from Bombay which is India. My brother come in his car and I got in. This is one experience which I would never, never never, never like repeated.

Nahda Bibi

As I sit here watching the local news on T.V., listening to another racial attack that has happened in South Yorkshire with my daughter, I realise how much prejudice she will go through in her life. As she is only five she can't understand that the colour of her skin offends some people.

She's only been racially abused once and the girl that said these things wasn't old enough to understand what she was saying and neither was my daughter.

Sometimes when I pick my daughter up from school I feel the mothers look at me and it's not a nice feeling. Some of them talk to me but I know they can't see past the colour of my skin. They talk to me because they think it shows they're not racist, but others accept me for a person.

I have been verbally abused many times on the street but I have never been physically attacked. As I've grown up I've learned to ignore it though while it was happening I was very afraid.

Me and my husband were both born in Sheffield so we are British citizens, but some people think because you're Asian you were born in a different country.

I believe that racial attacks aren't on the increase, as I think people are becoming more educated and seeing us for the people we are not for the colour of our skin. I hope by the time my daughter has children, racial attacks will be almost none.

Eizabeth Hilbert

There is power in such words beyond the fact of young people making language in an isolated British inner-city school classroom. It is in the power of becoming — becoming yourself and becoming others, and in the process becoming mindful of the struggle and stamina of others: never leaving yourself but at the same time entering others and making a welcome for others in yourself. It is what we need now to help our young people withstand the enclosing walls that the state-managed education changes are constructing between them, each to the other, and between them and the other human beings all over the world—and open wide the hope expressed by the Zimbabwean Dambudzo Marachera, 'to awaken in all things a community with what we experience ourselves .... we call it love.'[9]

Notes

1   *Sheffield Telegraph:*, 2 April 1992.
2   Sivanandan, A., *New Statesman and Society,* December 1991.
3   Berger, John, *Keeping a Rendezvous,* London, 1992.
4   Tagore, Rabindranath, *Glimpses of Bengal*, London, 1991.
5   Machell, Samora, 'Fazer da escola uma base para o povo tomar o poder' from *A nossa luta:*, Maputo, 1975.
6   Couto, Mia, *Voices Made Night,* London, 1990 and Magaia, Lina, *Dumba Nengue,* London, 1989.
7   This, and other work by Sheffield school students which follows, is from *Valley of Words*, an anthology of writing from Earl Marshal Comprehensive School, Sheffield, Sheffield, 1992.
8   Berger, John, op. cit.
9   Marachera, Dambudzo, *The Black Insider*, London, 1992.

'FAMILIAR AND HEROIC': HERSTORY AND THE INNER-CITY
(1995)

The Yemeni girl who wrote in the herstory of her mother's life that she had lived 'a very dramatic yet difficult life', touched the truth of the life-experiences of the women of the new British inner-cities. Drama and struggle: they certainly characterise the heart of the communities served by schools such as ours, and the mothers and grandmothers of our students have provided the heartbeat.

In his Victorian novel, *Henry Esmond* (which I studied at school for 'A' level English Lit.)—W. M. Thackeray declared that the primary content of history should be 'familiar rather than heroic'. The phrase and its polarities have stuck with me ever since my own school days, yet now I realise (and I have learned this from my own students), that the herstory of their mothers is both familiar and heroic, crossing borders of race, language and national culture.

The 'National Curriculum' hoisted upon all British schools through the 1988 Education Act makes the British state, and its male upholders through history, dominant and heroic. There is little room to study, know and affirm the lives and struggles of the working class people with family origins from many parts of the world, who compose the population of the inner-cities, and even less room for the particular stories of the women of these communities. It is a backward, nostalgic and sterile nationalism that governs the ideology of the National Curriculum view of history, completely opposed to the dynamic new internationalism that composes life and real experience in British inner-city neighbourhoods. It is that same narrowness of political view that seeks to impose Christianity in schools as the 'national' religion and the foundation of an renewed and clean 'morality' in a context that is vibrantly multifaith. It also ignores all languages spoken by English people other than Standard English, giving no curriculum recognition to other great languages that are the first languages of millions of British people; Urdu, Punjabi, Bengal, Turkish, Hindi or Arabic.

Yet it is this immediate organic knowledge of community, family and self that truly constitutes an understanding of history or herstory. It is a part of the making of a popular culture and at the centre of the process of self-realisation and community consciousness that leads to a struggling people's consolidation and development: that history and herstory belong to them. It also generates an understanding of neighbouring communities by its sharing within this human amalgam, how other working men and women in different contexts, locations and cultures have experienced similar dramas and struggles, how similar human lives are when all are working from aspiration and hope and seeking betterment and growth. It also affirms that a worthwhile curriculum cannot be arbitrarily imposed from outside a community's own experience. To do this is to kill stone-dead the creative possibilities for the generation of knowledge between teacher, student and parents. For a school's offer of knowledge to have integrity there must be a meeting between community and curriculum, with educational experience arising from the life struggles and achievements of the people whom the school serves. It is this curriculum rendezvous that a true telling of herstory creates.

Herstory and oral tradition

This herstory and its source material is primarily oral in character, multilingual in form and international in its context. To find permanence it needs to be gleaned by interview and transcription: by research and scholarship within the community where it is made. Jan Vansina, in his seminal book, *Oral Tradition as History*, emphasises that the 'verbal testimony' that is the basis of oral history, comes from the interview with the 'performer' who is providing the information. This interview, he asserts, is in itself a 'social process', and runs the risk of producing results that are 'minimal, often inaccurate and usually perceived as extorted under duress'—unless the interview situation itself is 'conducive to relations of trust and frank exchange.' What more trusting and close relationship between teller and recorder could exist than that between mother and daughter, or grandmother and daughter—speaking the same language, the language the daughter herself has learned from the mother? And when the content of herstory itself is the life-information being passed, often for the first time, from one generation to another, later to be passed as family tradition and inheritance by the daughter to her own children further down the chain of generations? The act of researching and recording herstory, transcribing and editing oral testimony, becomes education for consolidation of the bonds between parents and children, the affirmation of community life and the discovery of knowledge which is life-sustaining and identity-creating. For the working class student this can be the most important knowledge of all, knowledge conventionally ignored by the schooling process and the state-licensed curriculum which has other socializing priorities often completely at odds with her community's health, power and sustenance.

Thus a local 'herstory' campaign conducted primarily by daughters researching the lives of their mothers and grandmothers, is herstory as an act of trust by the teller, and proud, often surprised acceptance by the recorder, a family act which reaches outer ears and wider understanding when it is put alongside other lives and shared by classmates and schoolmates whose families have had experiences which have been in context and location entirely different, but often thematically very similar. Thus students in a northern English ex-industrial city move out of the 'National Curriculum', into the curriculum of their own family lives to write the life stories of their mothers from Pakistan, Yemen, Somalia, the Caribbean, Bangladesh, Sheffield and other parts of Britain. They are stories of lives of continuous work at home, in farms and factories, of frustrated education, of attempted domination by men—sometimes fathers or uncles, sometimes husbands, of suppression and rebelliousness, of marriage and childbirth, of war, migration and resettlement, of motherhood, grandmotherhood, reflection and understanding—all passed to the daughters and young women of another generation which they hope will enjoy the benefits and advantages that have come from their lifelong struggles.

A long recognition

For the daughters, the question 'where do I belong in all of this?', is a difficult and complex one. Sometimes born in their parents' homeland, sometimes born after emigration yet returned to their parents' home for long sojourns, living in a Muslim home and studying in a secular school and speaking two languages—one for each place, moving within cultural restrictions which other classmates, white and black have never experienced and cannot understand, experiencing racism, exclusion and cultural aggression, the sexist stereotyping of school and its teachers, boy classmates, fathers and brothers, the harassment of a male-dominated and white dominated world around them—for the black daughters faced by the experiences of their much-travelled mothers speaking of a life across two continents, there are shocks, surprises and realisations that leave much to ruminate upon. For white girls, hearing of these lives and sharing their documentation—lives which through location and culture seem so strange and different to those of their own mothers, it is a long recognition, beyond race, language and nationality to discover similarity and sisterhood in what to their own mothers and grandmothers, has been 'their' city, 'their' Sheffield. For theirs is often a long identity too, connecting back through generations of women who have lived in the same place, the same city.

> ### Sheffield Steel
> My mum was born in Sheffield
> As was my mam, Great Grandma too.
> 'It's the only place to live', says Mum
> And no other place would do.
>
> All the people here are friendly
> Strangers smile and say 'Hello'
> And they say the air is clearer
> Than it was some years ago.
>
> The rolling mills are gone now,
> A regret we all should feel,
> 'cos when Sheffield was mentioned
> Around the world, they'd all say steel
>
>   Zoe

The internal conflict fought out within the consciousness of many inner-city black girls about their dual-identity was set down by a 14 year old Yemeni girl in the poem that follows. Ironically she takes the title of a then-current pop-song and transmutes it to her own experience expressed through the words of a second language.

Shall I stay?
Shall I stay or shall I go?
Shall I stay in this country
Or shall I go to another?
I want to stay
I also want to go
It's difficult for me
And maybe it's difficult for you.
It's difficult for me, because
I don't want to leave
And it's difficult because I want to leave.
Maybe my feelings and your feelings are the same
They are the same only for one reason,
Because I love this country and I love the other country.
England and Yemen are my two countries
If I stay here I'll miss Yemen
And if I go to Yemen I'll miss England,
That's why it's difficult.
Tomorrow I'll be leaving this country
I'll be leaving this school
And all my friends and my teachers.
Where am I travelling to?
I'm leaving this country to go to my first country, Yemen.
You can't believe that my heart has divided into two.
One for England and the other for Yemen.

                       Safa Mohammed

In the midst of such uncertainty, the revelation of a mother's or grandmother's life and struggles can have an empowering impact. The daughter sees the strength and achievement of the mother—her stamina, as the foundation of family life for all the years the daughter can remember, and long before that. How does she apply what she learns from this 'familiar' history, these lessons of life told to her from her mother? How does she set out to creatively learn from them in her own young life, how do they charge her ambitions, frame her aspirations for her own education and the life ahead? These are vital questions at the heart of the herstory and its impact upon the education of the daughter in a society where opportunities are not equal, and where the odds may be stacked against her.

Work as herstory

The story told by all these mothers is first and foremost a story of work, from the earliest age, work. There is an alignment of experience here, whether on a farm in Kashmir, in a council flat or terraced house in Sheffield or living in a Yemeni village. Here is how a Yemeni girl has set down the years of child-work that were an integral part of her mother's life, and a reflection of the life of millions elsewhere in the world:

> At the age of 12 she had learned to cook, so she helped her sister with all the cooking and cleaning throughout the house. When she wasn't cooking she would help on the farm. She helped to sow the seeds, water the crops, and dig out the weeds. This work was terribly difficult as it all had to be done during the day, when the sun was at its hottest. But as time went on, she learned to live and work with sun. Everybody in the family had to help with the sowing, weeding and watering but the men did most of the work, as the women had other jobs such as bringing in water to the tank. The water came from a well. The wells were in the village. There would be about one well for each village. They never ran out because the villages were quite small and the population of these villages was not very big.
>
> Bringing the water in from the village was usually done by the women. The well was about a mile away from my mother's home. They would usually go in a group about 5,6,7, or 8 of them. They would take like a plastic barrel with them. When they got to the well, each one of them would wind the bucket down the well, bring it back up full of water and fill their barrel up. Then they would help each other by putting one another's barrel on their back. The walk home would be longer and harder. Each one of them would arrive home, hot, sweaty, tired and eager to have some rest, but they couldn't rest just yet as there was more work to be done.
>
> When the water had been fetched, the dinner cooked and eaten, and the farm had been seen to, then this was the time for rest. But to my mother this was the time to wash the family's clothes. They didn't have a washing machine. Actually they didn't have anything modern. They didn't have any fridges, no washing machines and even the cooker was just a little stove. They also had no taps and the water they drank was rain water. Because they had no washing machines all the washing was done in a metal tub. They would take the tub outside and do the washing outside.

Another Yemeni mother confirms this, adding more detail to the basic task of water-collection.

> When I was about nine years old I learned how to cook and how to get the water. You couldn't believe that I had to walk about 8 miles to get the water! I had to wake up at three or four o'clock in the morning to make the breakfast,

and then go to get the water. When it was about six o'clock I woke up all the family, and at about six or seven they had to go to the farm while I had to stay at home because at twelve o'clock I had to take the dinner I had cooked for them to the farm. And then I had to stay there to help with the work until about three-thirty. Then when I got home I had to work at many other things.

A Pakistani mother tells of the work of childcare that fell upon her when her mother became ill, and how this affected her schooling. She also tells of the intervals between work or time stolen from it, snatches of a childhood idyll, which gave her the opportunities to respond to and enjoy the beauty of the land where she was born.

Miss Akter (my mother) was born in the Punjab in Pakistan in 1953 and lived there throughout her childhood. Miss Akter spent most of her time bringing up her younger brothers and sisters. She had three brothers and three sisters. She was the oldest. Her father worked on the trains, serving food and her mother sewed clothes as a part-time job. So this left Miss Akter quite a big responsibility looking after so many children and going to school. Though education wasn't like it is nowadays, Miss Akter used to attend a mosque, there she would be able to learn to read the Koran and learn to read and write in Urdu. Miss Akter was taught quite well, but unfortunately she had to leave school, for when her last baby brother was born he was quite ill, and to top things up her father had gone to Greece for a short period of time. Both mother and child were quite ill and had to move into the local hospital, and so Miss Akter had to visit her mother regularly and look after her younger brothers and sisters. Luckily she had some friends and relatives to help her, but it was quite hectic for her older brother was only one at the time and the rest were quite young too. That must have been the hardest time in her life. Apart from that, her baby brother had diarrhoea and nappies weren't used as often, so she would have to get up in the middle of the night and take him to the toilet. She would also have to wash his dirty clothes if she didn't make it in time to the toilet.

Miss Akter had some pleasant times in her childhood as well. The village she lived in was beautiful, with open fields and streams. Miss Akter would spend her whole sunny days with friends running around in the open fields paddling in the streams. She also used to collect wood for the fire back home. She remembers once her mother told her to go and collect wood for the fire. So off she went, on the way she met up with some of her friends and so they all decided to play instead. They went far off into the forest and spent the whole day near the stream trying to catch fish with their hands. Meanwhile back home her mother was going frantic! She sent a message to her husband at work and told her neighbours to look out for her. Then towards the end of the day Miss Akter decided to stroll dreamily back into the village—six hours late and no word! I don't really want to write what happened next but you could probably guess. At this stage I asked my mum if she regretted doing that and she said no, but she deserved the punishment she received afterwards.

For the mother of a girl from Shiregreen in Sheffield, the work which came to her was not so different, and the burden of responsibility no less heavy—but the places to escape to held much more menace.

Because both parents worked all day, when school holidays came no-one was at home, so my mum had to look after her brothers. She had to keep a key which was attached to a piece of string that went around her neck. They wandered off anywhere, even dangerous places such as train lines and high bridges but their favourite place was the river. There used to be a tree trunk going from one side to the other and they used to play on that or try to catch tiddlers or have races with sticks or leaves. Her parents never knew where they went, and so my mum suspected that they didn't care about them.

My mum's mum then got a job which meant going early in the morning and so my mum had to make her brother's breakfast, which was usually porridge, this meant using the gas cooker which was very dangerous. She also had to make sure they were dressed and had everything they needed, as well as her own things.

In 1969, when my mum was 13, her sister was born, which put even a bigger burden on my mum. When she was only 2 weeks old my mum had to babysit for her at night while her mum and dad went to the pub. She even had the job of bathing and feeding her. Wherever she went she had to take her sister with her, she even went to her first Saturday morning disco at 18 months old.

And for this Bangladeshi mother, there is an intense pride in the recollection of the village of her girlhood. It is a pride in the efforts of her people to work, transform and humanise a flat and riverine landscape rendering it into both a beautiful and productive place to live:

I was born in Sylhet, a district in rural Bangladesh, in the north-east of the country. Where I was born was a fine and beautiful place, it had nearly everything one could expect. The place was extremely clean, with no litter laying around. Most of the people who lived in the village cared about the place very much and did their bit to keep it looking remarkably well and tidy—to me the people were like environmentalists. When one came to the village, one could see and smell the green grass and also smell the perfume from the different types of flowers. There were also ponds which had clean, clear water where one could see many diverse fishes, most of them were bright colours. The pond was extremely pretty with the water lilies and white pebbles down beneath the bottom, which appeared to look like pearls. Probably that was why the village was called Suna Pur (Village of Gold).

A frustrated schooling

For almost all these mothers, irrespective of place of life, formal education was a truncated or interrupted experience which for those who controlled their lives, only impeded continuous work. Shameem's mother, 'born in the mountains of Kashmir' in a two-roomed house 'in the middle of a grassy mountain,' seemed to live through a not unusual situation as far as school was concerned:

> There was a school nearby for the villagers, but she never really attended. She said 'What's the point? School will not do me any good, I'd get married anyway.' So she stayed home and did the house work and worked in the fields.

Thousands of miles away in Sheffield, the schooling of an English girl did not seem so different.

> When my mum was 6 she started Shiregreen school, and by the age of 10 they moved to a house at Middlewood but went to a school in Hillsborough. My mum didn't like school at all because she was afraid of being picked on as she was shy. She also thought the work was too hard and she was scared to ask for help. The teachers were very strict and once she got the cane for laughing at a teacher who slipped down in the snow. The school was a bus journey away and my mum, at just the age of 10, had the responsibility of taking her brothers an the bus to school and back home again. This was only the beginning of her responsibilities and chores.

And in Yemen too opportunities for girls' education were erratic and occasional and powerfully restricted in their curriculum; as the comments of these two mothers imply:

> At the age of seven, she was old enough to attend school. The school was an all girls school and was only ever open during certain hours in the day. In the morning the school taught one set of children and in the afternoon another. My mother sometimes vent in the afternoon. She couldn't go to school everyday as she had to help around the house or in the family farm. So I guess that's the reason why her Arabic literature and grammar isn't up to scratch.

> She went to learn at the age of eight but during that time there weren't schools like there are now. So she used to go to a mosque to learn the Holy Book (The Koran). This place was called Mallamah in Arabic, which means a place for learning the Koran.

For another Pakistani mother school became little more than a pretext for continuous rebellion. Her entire story, in fact reads as one act of protest after another, against marriage, work and beginning from her rejection of her mosque-school, and her preference for the free company of friends:

She had two best friends at this time, one was called Jamila and one was called Thazeem. Their parents used to send them to mosque in their own village and the teacher used to smack them because they would sometimes bunk school. When they used to go they didn't read. And they'd only go halfway to mosque and then they'd mess around everywhere.

Her uncle told the teacher that if she didn't arrive at the mosque, he was to go and find her. But even then she still wouldn't go. So the teacher told my mum's uncle to leave her at home for a week to make her read, and he said alright. But she still wouldn't read and instead of going to mosque with her friends, at night she went home with them. So they took her to another mosque, far away from her friends—about the same distance from here to town. But there was no one to play with there, so she still went to look for her same friends from the other mosque. She stayed with that second mosque for about a year and kept on meeting her friends. Then she finally left and could play with her friends all the time.

A Jamaican mother speaks of her own struggle for education, as a single parent who has never lost her aspirations and is striving to improve and broaden her life—but whose life experience gave her the most fitting and wise qualifications for a profession in the social services:

We lived in Birmingham for eight years before leaving to return to Sheffield, after I split up with the children's father. That a was particularly traumatic time for all the family, but it was unavoidable. There was an attempt made by my husband and I to patch up the marriage, but it did not work, and when we came to Sheffield we lived with my sister and her family. We moved into our house six months later and I worked full time at S. R. Gents in Sheffield for a year and a half until I joined the Family and Community Services as a home help.

Working full-time with children at school was very taxing. It was made slightly easier by my friend who cared for all the children before and after school until I returned in the evening. Working part-time for the Family and Community Services allowed me to take and collect the children from school. That was an ideal situation. I worked there for a year and a half. Then, through a desire to help the children cope better at school, I decided to do some evening classes in English and Maths. As I progressed, I began to enjoy studying again, and then I had to opportunity to enter for a new course at Granville, now Castle, College in 1986. It was wonderful that I got onto the course but It meant a lot of changes in the household. The children had to do a lot to help themselves, learning to do housework and washing clothes and dishes. This change carried on because I entered Sheffield Polytechnic in 1987, and because money was short, I worked in the evenings after college.

Donna, my eldest girl, was proving a great help with the younger children and it was possible for me to carry on with my degree course. My sister and mother both lent their support, but it was not an easy time. It was the time when the children were growing up with their own individual teenage problems. There were timers when studying and working proved too much, and the time I could spend at home with the children was very little. I began to think (wonder) whether it was worth it. I never stopped having these worries but at the same time I got on with the course. I felt that I had to make an effort to complete this thing I had started. The family had already taken so much stress and made such sacrifice for me to enable me to continue to study. I carried on despite the difficulties and my lack of time with the children. Couple with taking care of them, I was struggling with the difficulties of tackling work which was new to me. It was the desire to succeed and pay the children back for their help and encouragement that I went on to complete my degree in 1991.

I left the Polytechnic on July 12, 1991 and started work on July 15. It had been a very difficult six years, what with studying, working, and bringing up children. It paid off for me because I am in a good and worthwhile job. A lot of my family life suffered. However, we have survived that experience, but not without a great deal of struggle. I don't regret the studying, but it would have been easier of I hadn't had to do the two jobs of studying and bringing up a family at the same time.

Marriage: 'My husband's maid'?

Despite the wholly different conventions of marriage which affected the mothers interviewed by their daughters—marriage through 'free choice' or marriage 'arranged' by fathers—there are, amongst the tellers from both traditions, testimonies of constraint and subjugation, as well as companionship and shared struggle. Certainly for some Muslim girls conducting the interviews, there was a complex and nagging tension between the imposition of an arranged marriage and their own determination not to be propelled towards it—thus sometimes creating a dislocation of generations between teller and interviewer. A Bangladeshi student expressed the force of her rebellious feelings in this poem:

Living for myself
If they say I shouldn't have been born
If I say I shouldn't have been made!
If they say I am useless, because I'm a girl.
I'll prove to them, they are dead wrong!

Why should I live my life for them?
When I was made to live for myself!

Why shouldn't I be educated as my brothers have been?
Why shouldn't I have a proper job?
Why shouldn't I have the opportunity as they have?

I want to do what is best for me,
Not make a mess of my life.
I don't want to get married at the age of fifteen
and start a family at the age of sixteen.
But if only my parents understood that!

I don't want to live my life in a kitchen,
Being my husband's maid.
Thinking each time, why I am going through this hell?
Why should I cry myself to sleep each night?
And pray this nightmare would end!

And how could these sentiments be surprising when faced by the experience of women in her family?

Being a woman for some was a terrible lament, because men would consider you as being worthless or nothing compared to them. Even if a girl was exceedingly bright and more academic than her brother, yet she wouldn't have the opportunity to go on with further education. The parents wouldn't say to anyone about how clever and academic their daughter was because this would humiliate the son. It would always be the son at the top and the daughter right at the bottom. So while the daughter cooked, cleaned and pretended to be dumb, the parents would support and encourage their son to do well in his education.

For one Pakistani mother, marriage in the Kashmiri countryside came suddenly, without warning, made by the negotiation of others:

It was at the age of 17 when her parents decided to get her married. She had only seen her fiance once when they were engaged. Their engagement came about while her father was working in the shop and somebody pointed out to someone that they had a son in England at marriageable age. So the two men met and talked. The next thing my mother knew she was getting married.

And as soon as a son was born, the marriage was judged to be successful:

A year later after she was married, she gave birth to a boy. Everyone was overjoyed. It is said that if the daughter-in-law gives birth to a boy first, the house is blessed.

Similarly for a Yemeni mother, her marriage and its aftermath seemed to be constructed outside of her, through the will and decisions of elders:

When my mother's sister got married (my aunty) all the household responsibilities were given to my mum. By now she was nearly fifteen. When she was fifteen she got married. It was an arranged marriage. My father had seen my mother before. He had seen her while she was out doing the washing. He would hide somewhere, and stay there until she had finished, then he would go away. It was tradition for the groom to buy his wife. The groom would pay the bride's family some money and if her family thought he was suitable then they would get them married. Sometimes if a rich man offered to give the bride's family an awful lot of money so she could be his wife, then the family would also find him suitable. It was also tradition, that when the couple got married, the bride was to go away and live with her husband's family and to carry on the traditional customs, that was what my mother had to do. She went to live with her in-laws. They had five daughters and one son (my father). They lived in a neighbouring village also in Yafia, so when she went to visit her parents she didn't have to travel far, which was lucky as some girls who get married live miles and miles away from their original home.

A Bangladeshi mother tells a story about the arranged marriage experience of a girlhood neighbour and friend, Lila. To this mother she was 'like a childhood older sister ... a very kind and approachable girl. I always noticed that she had some conflict in her mind about what is right and what is wrong in life, maybe that was why I had enormous admiration for and envied her for who she was.' When Lila was 14, she heard the sudden news of her impending marriage:

It was only a week before the wedding that Lila came to know, and you can imagine how she felt. Terrified, heart-broken and frustrated she was, a girl at that age knew nothing really about men, sex or children. Mothers didn't actually talk to their daughters about these matters, they would find it uncomfortable or even humiliating to talk about them. So the results would be 'do it, and face it the hard way'.

Then when it came to her own marriage, she too was 'shocked and terrified' when she was told so suddenly and sharply by her father that 'she was to be wedded to his friend's son, Farooq. Everyone was saying how lucky I was to be marrying a man living in Britain, with so much money. I was gradually getting my hopes up until I was shown the photo of my future husband. As soon as I saw Farooq I felt as miserable as before. He was short, fat and unattractive. His eyes had undesirable looks and his smile showed nothing. He was posing with his flared jeans and bright red shirt which made his belly stick out. His hair was long and bushy, it seemed he never had cut it. There was nothing I liked about him, he was just undistinguished. I just thought to myself, 'Oh my God! How could I spend my life with a man like that?'

And the day of the wedding was soon upon her, and soon gone:

> ... my grandmother told me about the 'big night', she told me things I shouldn't do, like tell about the boys I knew in the past, cry all the time and many other things. After she finished telling me all these things the wedding sari was put on me, which was extremely beautiful and expensive. Then the orna (a long scarf worn over the head) was put on me, which was also red, but with tinsel.
>
> After the wedding feast was over, it was time for me to go. Everybody was crying to see me go, I was crying too. Outside, a shwari (a covered sedan chair for carrying brides) was waiting to bear me away to my new village, Tagim Pur.

And for the English girl of the sixties, her life also restricted by family responsibilities, 'love' and then marriage comes hurrying to her through the one weekly opportunity she has for her own freedom:

> She was allowed to go out only one night a week with her work friends and one of those nights is when she met my dad. He was with his friends and he kept looking at her. Everytime he caught her eye he would do something to make her laugh. Some people don't believe in love at first sight, but for them it did happen. They saw each other everyday and even sent love letters to each other. She was 17 and they got engaged after 4 months and got married a year after they first met. They moved to Willoughby Street at Page Hall. It had no hot water and no bathroom and they only paid £5.00 a week rent. They had to go to my dad's grandma's for a bath. After a few weeks of being married my mum found out she was pregnant, which was my brother. Two months before he was due to be born my dad lost his job as a postman. He was out of a job for nine months before he got his job at Tinsley Wire, where he still works. All he has to do is thread bobbins of wire on to a machine that welds the crosswise wires together.

Drudgery, isolation and enterprise

The sense of alienation and boredom in a father's work which this young herstorian records, is reflected through much of the work experience of the young women who were now so suddenly also working wives. The post-school work, for example of this Sheffield mother, mirrors the work done by two young Yemeni wives whose testimonies follow on directly—the same sense of drudgery heightened by the isolation of being far away from their own families, living with in-laws who are in a prime situation to exploit and abuse them:

She left school at 15 with no qualifications and she got a job in a scissor warehouse, she had to clean all the dirt off the scissors, make sure they cut properly, then pack them up in boxes ready to go to the shops. For this she got £7.00 a week, £3.00 of which went to her mum. She worked there for three years.

My mother was given a room in a three storey flat, which belonged to her father-in-law and his brothers. The ground floor was for his grandfather's youngest brother and his wife, and the second floor was for his second brother and his family. The third floor was my mother's and father's.

Not long after she'd got married, she had to start helping her eldest sister-in-law with the cooking, cleaning and all the other types of domestic jobs. It took a while before she settled in, because her in-laws weren't treating her as fairly as the others. She felt very awkward there as she was the only stranger living there. Everybody else knew everyone and it took her awhile to adjust herself to their way of life, which was in a way similar to her with her parents.

Because she was the eldest of the young women she had to do the cleaning and the washing. She also had to fetch water from the wells. Her sisters-in-law accompanied her for these as they needed a lot of water. She also had to help with the farming. This farm grew coffee beans, gat (which is a type of plant which the men usually chew, while they are relaxing. It is a sort of a soft unharmful drug which only causes headaches afterwards) and they also grew corn. These were important crops and without these crops most families wouldn't be able to survive. The men helped with the farming, but they usually had to keep themselves busy with the building.

When I was fifteen I got engaged and when I was sixteen I got married— but the wedding wasn't as good as I expected it to be. My husband took me to stay with his family and he went back to England. One month later I got pregnant.

When I had my baby I had it at home because at that time there was no hospital near our village. It was a very difficult life. I was 35 miles away from my family and at that time there was no transport, you just had to walk—it was much more difficult for me then when I lived with my own family.

For a young Pakistani wife too, the housework in the in-law house became her assigned role:

Because she was the eldest in-law, it meant that she was given the responsibility for the house. One thing she hated doing was lighting the oven and then sticking the chapatis on it. She told her mother-in-law that she'd do all the housework, but not that because it would burn her arms.

For Lila, in her Bangladeshi village, the influence of her mother-in-law became pernicious, and finally fatal. Her friend recounts:

> Her husband Koshin was nice to her and respected her, but there was one person who made her life not worth living—her wretched mother-in-law. She did everything she could to make Lila's life a misery and everyone to hate her. After a year passed, Koshin grew to hate her. He began to find different excuses to beat her brutally with a steel rod, several times causing severe damage to her body. After hearing her screams the village people came to her rescue. But it was too late—too late for anything, Lila was dead. At the age of just 16, so helpless and defenceless she was slaughtered by her own husband.

A young English wife, having angered her parents by her choice of husband, also moves into her in-laws' house and found herself being its painter and decorator as well as housekeeper:

> A year passed by and they both decided to get engaged. This didn't really please Betty's parents especially since he was twenty years older, a Roman Catholic and had three sons. Not that they would affect Betty as they lived with his mother. But still despite the fact Betty's parents objected, they married at Saint Catherine's Roman Catholic Church on the 14 November 1953.
> Betty's early years of marriage were quite hectic, they moved into Dennis' house on Barngreave Road. The house was quite large and needed a lot of decorating and attention, which Betty managed to do mostly by herself. In fact she carried on decorating and working right up until her daughter was due to be born.

This grandmother had found herself a job as a school-leaver which must have touched the depths of alienation. As her granddaughter writes: "After the war was over, Betty, only at the age of fourteen, started work. She remembers her first job vividly, which was painting spots on dominoes ..."

There was also another aloneness—a frightening feeling of being alone in a new and strange country, which arrivant mothers experienced as their husbands were working long hours and they felt trapped in houses which must have seemed like prisons—as with this mother who found herself living in Darnall, in north-east Sheffield, with her husband working double shifts at British Steel:

> When my Mum arrived she said that it all seemed tight—that was probably because she had lived in open fields ... She couldn't go out alone on buses. She could only go out when her husband (my Dad) returned from work. At home, my Mum cried for about a month after coming from Pakistan, because she was lonely. She had no one to talk to. She couldn't speak the language so she couldn't make friends. She didn't know her way around. She was scared

to go out in case she got lost. My Mum just sat in front of the window and watched people go by.

Another English grandmother tells of her life in domestic service, the fate of almost an entire generation of teenage working-class girls. 'It was a hard life,' she recounts, 'because we had to do everything we were told to,' with the people of the house 'always having to be referred to as master and mistress'. She continues, remembering the terrible undervaluing that girls endured:

There was no answering back, if we did we would have been sacked and no reference given for another job.

In those days father and the male in the family used to think all the women should do was to go into domestic service, leave to get married and continue drudgery into their married life: e.g. have children, look after them one hundred per cent, wait hand and foot upon their husbands, have their noses to the grindstone and not expect too much pleasure, if any at all. It was all hard work and no money in those days.

The tedium of domestic work is described in grim and realistic detail by this grandmother as she tells of the task of laundering:

There were no modern facilities for washdays. I had two zinc tubs for washing and rinsing clothes. I had a posser but some women had a dolly-peg. I put some clothes in one tub, used the posser to help release some of the dirt in the clothes. After this I used to put the rubbing board in the tub and rub each garment with snap on it. This done, I put the other clothes into the other tub and rinsed them well.

The next part of the process was to boil the whites. I was very lucky to have a gas boiler but some women had fire boilers—they had to be up early to light the coal fire because it took a long time to boil ready for the clothes. I would rinse them thoroughly, if they were ready I would take them in wooden troughs for rinsing and mangling, starch any that needed starching then hang them out to dry if the weather was fine ...

Yet these accounts compare starkly with the working life of a Pakistani woman, an arrivant in England, who had the will (and lack of opposition from her husband) to pursue her own career interest. 'She started taking up a textile course and started sewing Pakistani clothes,' recounts her daughter. She also, 'decided to take up Adult Education classes and was taught how to read and write in English properly'. From these beginnings she developed her own home-based enterprise which rescued her from domestic drudgery and gave her a new pride in her skills and achievements in work, spurred on by the achievements of her own children:

She watched her children grow up. She became very happy and proud of them as they brought good school reports home and certificates. Mrs. Rashid then started sewing clothes again and made a good little business, as she designed and sewed clothes. Her good quality clothes attracted a lot of people and she had customers all over Sheffield and Rotherham. Mrs. Rashid was very pleased with this and took a great deal of pride in her work.

Many wars

For these women there are many explosions in their lives—marriage, separation from husbands, emigration, children, needing to retain links with parents and family in the homeland, confronting racism and sexist oppression, the barriers of language, the struggles towards equality—and war.

For this Yemeni mother, her war was an anti-colonial war, fought on the streets of Aden against a British occupying army. For her young teenage husband, this war meant blindness—for his wife it meant rebuilding two lives, almost from the beginning. Her daughter finds her own poetry-in-prose to describe her mother's struggle:

At that time Aden was very dangerous because of the British occupation, which had started in 1838. So the people of Aden suffered a lot.

After two years of fighting the British army, the man who wanted to marry my mother got blinded when he was fighting with my grandfather against some British soldiers. They shot my father in his eyes. At that time he didn't want anything from his life because he had lost his sight. He thought that his life was finished. They brought a doctor for him but he couldn't do anything for my father. So he became a blind man at the age of 16.

So my mother got married to my father and she was just 13 years old. She was very young to get married but she hadn't any choice. She was so young to understand the life of marriage. Being a woman, a woman who was going to share a life with a man who couldn't see anything at all, that time was the hardest time for both of them—for my mother and my father. She couldn't understand him because she was still very young and he couldn't understand himself either becoming a blind person now for the rest of his life, living in the darkness all the time, not knowing what was going on around him. They shared some very hard, sad moments in their lives.

But she was a real woman because she was taking care of my father very much. She understood how he felt and she did her best to change him into a real man and a lucky man like he had been before, and better than before. At first he used to shout at her and beat her because she was the person who was with him all the time. For when you lose your eyes what can you do without them? It was very hard for him and for her too. But the years went past and this woman was very lucky to change her husband to a person who can see with his heart, not just with his eyes.

This was a war in the past where the enemy was the colonialism of Britain. Another mother cast her memories back to her uncle's experiences in the First World War, and another anti-colonial struggle, in Ireland, where he, as a British soldier, found himself categorised with a rebellious people merely because of his name:

> I was not alive in any real war, but it did affect my family.
>
> My father's brother fought in the First World War. Wilf was 20 years older than my father. My father's mother died when he was small, so my Grandfather could not look after my father. So at the age of 8 or 9 he was sent to a boys' home. Then my father's dad died when my father was 13 so then he was shipped off to Canada to another boys' home. During this time my father's brother was sent home for a convalescent period, and then Wilf was sent off to Ireland for the Easter uprising, where he met his wife Cassie. He didn't see much of the action though, because he was kept in Dublin nick for having an Irish name, but by the time he had been investigated it was all over, so he was sent back to Sheffield.

For this daughter, it was a realisation of the origin of her own Christian name, who had carried it before her, and in what circumstances.

But for most white Sheffield girls, their families' most direct link back to war was a war against fascism, felt strongly in the huge manufacturing 'steel city' of Sheffield, the target of a horrific Nazi blitz in December 1940. One of the girls' grandmothers recalled her own memories of the war against Hitler, which broke out when she was eight years old:

> This of course interrupted her early schooling years and amongst other things caused everyone's education to suffer.
>
> Betty doesn't seem to remember too much about the beginning of the war, only the rationing e.g. an average family of six might be rationed to:
>
> 1/2 lb butter a week
>
> 2 lb sugar a week
>
> 1 8 oz pkt of egg powder a week etc.
>
> So because of this her parents had to close their grocer's shop and move back to the rear of their barber's shop.
>
> The next thing she remembers was her oldest brother, Tommy, being called up into the army. Times were hard for the Williamson family as like many others during the war. They all missed Tommy very much and loved him coming home on his short leaves.
>
> A year passed by, in which time things had become more serious. The Sheffield steel industry was making armoured plating for tanks, which made it more and more likely that Sheffield would be bombed. So Betty's parents sent Betty and little brother Harry into the countryside to live with their aunt.

This procedure was quite normal in a lot of families and was known as EVACUATION! By this time Betty was about nine or ten, old enough to know what was going on. She hated life with her Aunt and soon became homesick.

Eventually she persuaded her aunt to let her and Harry return home, but they hadn't been home very long when Sheffield was blitzed.

On that first terrible Sunday night, her family was awakened by the dreadful sirens piercing their ears, this could only mean one thing, the German planes were on their way. The whole family hid down the cellar, scared, cold and not daring to speak.

After the bombing was over everyone came out of their hideouts to take a look at the damage. There were windows blown out and furniture smashed, not to mention the dust and debris everywhere. Of course this was soon cleaned up, but only for the same thing to happen the following Thursday.

For other mothers war represented something ghastly in the present, in the centre of their families' lives. Some of the newest Sheffielders were refugee families from Somalia's civil war. Their sufferings under the tyrannical rule of Siad Barre—whose army and air force had destroyed their cities of Hargeisa and Burao in northern Somalia—had been narrated with a terrible nakedness by one local Somali mother:

At night the government troops came back to some areas of the city and they slaughtered everyone they could round up including women, children and elderly people. They smashed water cisterns and swore at everyone: 'We know you were shouting out your support for the SNM and the enemies of the Somali government!'.

As the bullets came without stopping many people ran from their small houses made of natural materials, as they gave no cover. The bullets came through the walls. They asked for shelter in the homes with stone walls. Our house sheltered ten families, which included a lot of children. We couldn't refuse—we were all relatives, all suffering under the same terrible pressure.

Later, when houses began to collapse under the ceaseless bombardment, people had to run openly in the streets to try to escape the guns, and had to flee and completely evacuate the war-torn city. As we fled we saw the dead bodies lying in the street and beneath the rubble of the broken and ruined houses.

The fugitives were town-dwellers, they had no idea where to go. There were mothers with their babies, pregnant women, old people, sick people. Most of them were barefooted, they had had no time to find their shoes, or wore simple, thin sandals which were soon destroyed and torn to pieces as they stepped through the thorny bushes. There was hardly any food and drink, and some pregnant women actually gave birth when they were on the run. They all had to move fast to escape the government soldiers, but they also had to find places where there was water. The armed forces were in pursuit and started to catch and kill some of the people, even though they were innocent civilians. They didn't see us as any different from the SNM fighters. They were only interested in massacring us—the Isaak people—on the direct orders of the government.

In our own house the artillery bombardment had badly damaged the roof. Then my brother-in-law said we must get out. He pulled the hands of my daughter and I ran after him, pushing a wheelbarrow which contained food, clothes blankets and drinking water. After a terrible journey across the country we came to Wadhan, a water point. We began to settle down there under the trees, using sheets to shelter from the sun. Nomads were also there, and had brought their animals for watering. Then in the early morning the government army arrived, approaching us from a dried up river bed the other side of us. They opened fire, killing all whom that they could see—people and animals.

They killed my mother and two other female relatives. In all sixty people were killed on that occasion at the water point, then they went to the nearby village and killed everybody there, except a few who fled into the bush.

Then they looted all our valuable belongings and those of the villagers. They smashed everything left behind, including cooking pats and water containers. And this did not only happen to Wadhan, but in other places all over northern Somalia.

This particular herstory became a very effective educational resource throughout the school, and was read by many classes as a vital background text towards an understanding of the struggle of Sheffield's Somalis and the extent of their tragedy and ordeal during the previous months. That such experiences were now in the heart of Sheffield and its people came as a shock to many students, as they marvelled at their Somali classmates and their families' powers of endurance and stamina. When the school began a campaign to raise money to re-equip the shattered schools of Hargeisa and Burao where many of the Somali students in the school had attended before the civil war and their flight from their country—there was very strong support from all sections of the school population. Much of this was due to the understanding the students had found in testimonies such as the one above.

Resistance and justice

Throughout these herstories were scattered incidents and reflections on justice, oppression and the women's urge towards equality. A Yemeni mother asked the fundamental question, arising from the relationships that surrounded her in her family:

There were twelve people in our family—five sisters, four brothers and my wonderful Mum and Dad, and me of course. I was the oldest child so I had to do the hardest things, because at that time in my country when girls were over ten years old they had to do everything on their own, the mother's work was to do the farming and nothing else. The father had to do nothing! What he had to do was stay at home doing nothing just like a king! And that's what made me very mad because I don't think that there is any difference between a man and a woman. I think that we are all humans and there is nothing, nothing different between us. Don't you think so too?

All the time there are acts of resistance to this inequality, a refusal to accept it—as in the testimony of this young Pakistani wife:

My mum used to go swimming before she was married and she did the same after her marriage, but my dad didn't like it. So he hit her with a stick, and whenever she went from home to her uncle's house my dad used to follow and watch her wherever she went. Then one day he told her to milk the cows. She didn't want to so she ran off somewhere and they were looking for her for nine hours before they found her. She kept on doing this for three days and my dad didn't like it, so he sent her back to her uncle's house. She stayed there for about three weeks then my dad brought her back home and didn't talk to her for a week.

And this rebelliousness and attraction to justice expresses itself in opposition to other forms of oppression. Here an English mother refuses to act 'normally' and befriends a gay workmate. Despite the pressurising of peers and the scorn of others with whom she works, she refuses to let go of a warm and generous relationship:

I met my first homosexual friend at Boots. His name was Morris, he worked for EMI Record Company. He came from Leeds, he was Jewish. He used to come to Boots because he was a Rep for the Record Company. He used to take me out for lunch every Tuesday. We used to go to the Silver Dragon in Rotherham, Wellgate. He was a very nice fella, he used to buy me lovely Christmas and birthday presents.

My friends used to say, 'Uhh how can you go out with a puff!' I told them they didn't know what they were missing.

The same mother told of another struggle at her workplace, this time for a betterment of women's conditions at work and the right for married women to be employed under equal terms to those who were unmarried. Again there is the same determination to see justice, to see women advance and unjust laws and ways to be changed:

Boots was the first place against whom I took Union action, for a stupid law they brought out, the firm themselves brought out. Well, the Head firm said that no matter how long a person had worked there, if they got married they got the sack. It was their policy in future not to employ married women. But there were already married women working there who had previously been employed. But the thing was if these women had been employed for 6 months they would not get the sack. But if a girl had worked there from being

16 and then at 21 she was getting married, that gave her 6 years employment, she would still be sacked. So I told them they could not do it. So they threatened me with the sack if I brought the Union in, so I told them they had no grounds to stand on. But really it made no difference to me, I was not planning on getting married, I thought it was totally unjust and unfair.

This was a struggle waged by a courageous woman. The story told by the Somali refugee mother who reaches Sheffield with her children, finds herself in a council flat, isolated threatened, subject to local council bureaucracy" racist abuse and cruelly mocked and tortured by unknowing children, throws down a challenge to all who read it to find the same determination to struggle against the prejudice and ignorance that are causing this woman's agony:

So we could relax a little, but the English language was a huge barrier for us. We needed an interpreter for everything, even for shopping, we felt entirely dependent. We were offered a temporary flat, so we went to Sheffield Housing Department to sign the tenancy. I asked the Area Housing Office not to put me into that tenancy, but they insisted, telling me that I could apply for a house later on. Then we applied to the DHSS for a Community Care grant to furnish the flat. After a long time we were told we weren't eligible, so we appealed. Meanwhile, our children had got colds, and two of them became sick and were hospitalised at the Children's Hospital. I had become very depressed, thinking about all these new problems with the bureaucracies.

Finally we got a grant and moved to the other tenancy. But then we got a letter from the Council about a 'double rent', telling us we owed them from the first tenancy. When we said, 'But we couldn't move into the first tenancy, it had no furniture,' they answered: 'That is not our problem".

Apart from all this we were hearing continuous bangs at our door—even at midnight, which made us very nervous. On another occasion a letter arrived from someone telling us to get out of the place, and we found graffiti outside, which really increased our tension and made us feel humiliated. My husband tried to fight back physically against these people, but I reminded him he shouldn't look for trouble as we weren't there to cause conflict. It is only a matter of time. When our country becomes free again, we will go.

Sometimes children outside make what sound like cartridge explosions, and it makes me think back to the bombardment in Burao. I stand up immediately, because I am so startled, but then I remember I am here, not in Somalia.

At least the council rehoused us to another part of Sheffield, which is a little calmer. But the Housing Department still deducts money from the Income Support, and this makes a depressing situation for us, a family of six. But we have the Somali Community Association to help and support us, and I am also gradually learning the English language here. I have still got some of my children at refugee camps in Ethiopia, but during my stay in Sheffield I have managed to bring over a daughter and son to be with my other two daughters who came into Britain with me.

The story of another brave woman who struck out for justice in her life was told by this Bangladeshi mother. Soon after her marriage she discovered she had become her husband's third wife. 'I was upset and frustrated," she recounts, 'but there was little I could do then, carrying his child'. This husband became a faraway figure, working in Sheffield, England, as she brought up her son, Aziz in Sylhet. She reflects sympathetically about the Bangladeshi men who took his leap to work and live in another country:

> There were many men from Sylhet who went to work in the steel industry in the Lower Don Valley. They mainly did hard and arduous work in some of the most unclean and unhygienic places, just to earn money for the family back in their home land.

But her husband, unlike most, sent her no remittances: "He thought we had enough money to live on, and he always relied on his brother's money.'

Eventually he sent for her and their son. After coping with the emigration requirements of her own country, she came to the time of leaving, and the fear, confusion and insecurity she would feel on the other side:

> It was nine o'clock at night at Dhaka Airport. This was my first time seeing an airport. There were many people coming and going. My father and many other relatives came to see me and my son off. Our journey an the plane was frightening, but very exciting, especially for Aziz who loved every minute of it. On October 18 1978 we arrived. We landed at Heathrow Airport very early in the morning. There was no one to help us, we waited for hours in patience but still there was no sign of anyone. The immigration people asked many questions. Before I left home father had told me many things about immigration, and I tried to memorise these like a bird. I was confused, terrified and angry, and on my first day everything was such a state. I didn't know the people, the language or the country ...

Staying with her husband's cousin Saleh, in Southall, she was soon to experience the intensity of British racism, '... in the homes, streets at work and at school, almost everywhere. Skinheads used to go round-beating up any black people they saw. There were big gang fights and when the police were involved the blacks were left with all the blame.'

She experienced all the emotion of the infamous events of April 1979 when the Metropolitan Police held Southall in siege and attacked a demonstration against racism, causing the death of a London teacher:

A man named Blair Peach, a white anti-racist, was brutally killed by police after their intervention in the demonstration. Blair was described by some of the people as a man full of love and care, who looked at people as one instead of their colour. He was a man with strong dignity and full of vitality. Even though I never met Blair, I knew he was a man with a brave mind who died fighting for us. Saleh had gone to the demonstration with friends from the local community. He said that when he had heard that Blair was killed everything appeared upside down. When I saw people crying because of his death, I knew how much this man, who abhorred racism, meant to them.

Eventually called to Sheffield by her husband she found him 'redundant, like so many others.' Unemployment made his attitude to her even more negative and hostile, increasing the turmoil inside her. Soon his behaviour became uncontrolled and brutal, as 'the way he treated and beat me, it was more like I was a thing than a person. Sometimes I wished and prayed I was just buried alive. Even that would have been better than the torture I faced.'

Her very close friendship with a white married couple, her close neighbours, saved her life one night when her husband attacked and wounded her badly. This couple had already impressed her. The woman was 'caring and cordial' and her husband presented an example she had never been before, although her husband dismissed him as a 'wimp and a queer':

When I used to visit them, I used to see Peter doing the housework, like ironing, cleaning and cooking. I used to be so impressed by this man that I used to talk about him to my Bengali girlfriends.

She made her decisive act of rebellion when she left her husband, going to live with her English teacher in a neighbouring city. 'Even though my community knew what I had faced, they still thought I should go back to my husband,' she tells, adding that the flood of scandal and rumours that followed her accused her of being 'immoral' and full of 'sin'. Yet now secure by herself, bringing up her child, eventually qualifying as a social worker and grasping her independence, 'I have proved to myself that I can do something on my own two feet, and as a woman, I don't need a man to survive.'

Empowerment and emulation

These are extracts from upwards of two hundred herstories transcribed by students, of their mothers' and grandmothers' lives from an inner-city neighbourhood in north-eastern Sheffield in 1992. They are often testimonies of self-critical wisdom, ('For the bad things she had done and the bad times of her life, were lessons she had learned') as well as factual documentation of how an international community came to be made and composite in a small corner of the earth, in an inner-city neighbourhood of an ex-steel producing city in England. Such a small place, indeed, yet also a microcosm and expression of the 'immense cultural heterogeneity of a society that draws its cultural traditions from all over the world'.

Yet coming from the classrooms of the school in the heart of that same community, they are also more than this. These herstories had helped to empower both teller and recorder with the events of the past, had helped to make life make sense, helped to make the build-up of ordinary lives a part of an extraordinary canvas of achievement and community realization of its own resources and experience. This is a part of the development of a community's critical literacy, when it documents and becomes conscious of its rich diversity and amalgamated strength, and uses its local school as its means to reach this.

For the young women school students of the community—and for its boys too, who see and become conscious of their girl classmates' gathering confidence, as well as the struggles, privations and huge stamina of their mothers, and grandmothers—this diversity and strength can arrive like a revelation. In a proud, unabashed assertion of independent womanhood with the life herstory as its proving and affirmation, there are many lessons and insights for the entire community. The sense of witness, and living *educatively* towards reasons, conclusions, wisdom and understanding of a human's own life and its importance for others, is what expressed through this herstory, as set down in the concluding statements of this Bangladeshi mother:

> I shall finish the story of my life here. I have not written about my experience because I am against my religion or arranged marriages, but to tell you how strongly I am against men who force their daughters to marry. In all cultures, laws are in fact man-made, and force has no place in Islam. Men who force their daughters into marriage express their domination, ignorance and error and fail to be good Muslim fathers. I just wish to tell parents, before making any decision, to take everybody's thoughts and feeling into account. Many of our girls, like myself, conform to their parents' wishes simply because they do not want to appear disobedient and argumentative against their parents.
>
> I also think that no woman deserves to be treated the way I was, confused, trapped and terrified. Men should realise that women have their individuality and should learn to respect their wives and other women. Happiness depends upon understanding and friendship between husband and wife. The world is changing and with it our life-styles. We women need to change our attitude to life, otherwise men will continue to take advantage of us.

Yet the empowering had particularly affected the young women who were learning about the lives and struggles of the other, older women closest to them. Shortly before the herstory project was launched at the school, a number of its girls had bravely come forward and protested about a particular teacher who had been sexually harassing them over a long period. The school acted decisively and the teacher was suspended. Yet fear of what their community and school might think of them, a feeling of powerlessness and inner resignation had stopped them from complaining and protesting before and prompted them to truant school to avoid his classes. He was a man, he was a teacher, he represented power and authority—what could they do? Who would listen to them? 'We were only pupils and he was a teacher," wrote one girl, it was 'his word against ours'. 'Sometimes I wanted to get up and punch him but I knew that he was a teacher, he was bigger than me and no one would believe me. I could not tell anyone ...' It is a part of the curriculum responsibility of the school to challenge such feelings of powerlessness and unconfidence, particularly among its girl students. One girl answered directly through a poem which expressed a proud refusal to be dominated by any men in her life:

> I pose a serious threat to men—
> Through my work, lifestyle and manner.
>
> I am not locking my hands or mind
> I am not bowing or begging you, man!
> I am not going to be destroyed by you,
> Are you man, sad or disgraced?
>
> I am not your pleasure or comfort,
> I am not queen of the material world.
> I am not in your mind, though or life—
> Does all this truth anger you?
>
> I am not selling my body to you, man!
> Remember I'm no longer your whore,
> Remember I am not a sucker anymore.
>
> I pose a serious threat to men,
> Through my work, lifestyle and manner
> Because I am a woman.

The herstories had illustrated that the women, the mothers, were the makers of experience, the creators of community life. In doing so they had created new scope and inspiration for the daughters to emulate that experience by applying it to their own aspirations. All those qualities that the mothers had demonstrated and the achievements of life founded on those qualities—from courage to tenacity, from rebelliousness and rejection of patriarchy to enterprise and stability, could now be passed on and creatively applied by their daughters. And the sharing of these experiences, reading them out in classrooms, discussing them and finally publishing them together in a book which became a women's collective autobiography of an multi-racial, internationalist inner-city neighbourhood—its roots, formation and development—gave an image and example of cohesion to a large number of individual lives which had come together from many places in the world to one neighbourhood in a northern English inner-city.

In her herstory one of the Pakistani mothers described to her daughter how as a small child, she would follow her mother everywhere, and proudly try to copy all her mother's skills in the tasks that she did every day.

At this young age she used to like to copy everything her mother did. When her mother went down to the stream to do the washing so would she, and when her mother collected water from the clear fresh springs so would she. All the neighbouring women used to praise her abilities. And she used to like showing off.

Emulation, of course, is not copying. But it is applying skills learned from others, putting them to work in entirely new contexts, transferring them to new challenges and endeavours—following new paths using the excellence and confidence you have learned from others in study, work and struggle—particularly from those closest to you who have inspired you. It is at the heart of motivation and education, and its mechanisms should be the engine of our schools. As Maurice Bishop of Grenada declared, emulation is a recognition 'of the inventiveness and power' of those working around you, and is 'the seed which brings the fruit of excellence'. For in our school's community too, from the life-work and excellence of the mothers will come the achievement of their children to break out of systems of conservatism and patriarchy—and from the knowledge of the huge capacity and creativeness in their mothers' lives and herstories, will arrive the power of the daughters.

Notes

1. Vansina, Jan, *Oral Tradition as History*, James Currey, London 1985.
2. From *Valley of Words*, Earl Marshal School, Sheffield 1992.
3. See Apple, Michael, *The Politics of Official Knowledge,* Routledge, New York 1993 and Searle, Chris, *The World in a Classroom*, Writers and Readers, London 1977.
4. Searle , Chris (Ed) *In Nobody's Backyard : Maurice Bishop's Speeches,* Zed books, London 1984.

CURRICULUM AND COMMUNITY   (1995)

The Thatcherite conservative restoration in Britain signalled its intentions towards educational restructuring in 1988 with the passage of the Education Reform Act and the words of its conductor, Secretary of State for Education Kenneth Baker, who proclaimed that 'the age of egalitarianism is over.' Four years later and the government of John Major was moving still further, with the Prime Minister telling teachers from the podium of the 1992 Conservative Party Conference 'not to waste their time on the politics of gender, race and class', but to get on with buttressing a market system of education, preparing their students for a prescribed National Curriculum and faithfully testing their imbibing of it at the ages of seven, eleven, fourteen and sixteen—while having both eyes fixed upon their schools' progress up the examination league tables.

A disastrous scenario, one might surmise, for progressive teachers and those schools genuinely determined to serve their students and communities. Yet by the end of the academic year of 1992-3 many of the priorities and plans of the Conservative government and its latest minder of education—the picturesque and frenetic John Patten—were in ruins. Teachers and headteachers throughout Britain were boycotting national tests for their primary and secondary aged students, ignoring the 'orders' of the command curriculum and rejecting the identity of being, as the American educationalist Michael Apple has put it, the 'factory hands' of the classroom, 'whose duty it is to carry out mechanically and unquestioningly the ideas and orders of those clothed with the authority of position' in the reconstructed market place of state education, a market place which was also revealing that large numbers of mainly inner city school-age students (66,000 of them, according to a MORI poll on the BBC 'Panorama' programme *Out of Class*) were being set aside as soiled goods and permanently excluded from school—thus getting no education at all and undermining the founding principle of British education: compulsory education for all.

The reversals forced upon state education right across Britain—but felt most severely in its inner cities—threatened to sever curriculum from community and re-impose an utterly alienated perspective and construct of knowledge. This was coming after the efforts of many teachers during the previous two decades had sought to reconcile what is taught in inner city schools with the real lives of those with whom they shared their classrooms, and to reject models of streaming and constant competitive testing, developing instead more accurate, humane and motivating means of student assessment. During that period progressive teachers had worked to use education to give authority to the life experience and intellectual strength of ordinary working people and their communities, opposing a hegemonic view of state-licensed knowledge that locked both student and teacher up in an alienated and oppressive framework of someone else's curricula, and introducing what Edward Said has called 'contrapuntal' perspectives of class, culture, race and gender within which students could make their own investigations, insights and choices.

Although these approaches have taken a battering since 1988, they still survive and are alive and kicking out of their carapaces in many of Britain's schools. Teachers are discovering that the potentially deadening effects of the National Curriculum's handed-down teaching which threatens to 'factoryise' both themselves and their students, need to be opposed head-on in the classroom. As the Iranian woman poet Simin Belbahani wrote: 'to stay alive, you must slay silence', and no words could be more apt for the curriculum struggle now facing British teachers. For our schools must slay silence too.

To re-couple curriculum and community, to show that there is a vibrant and life-giving knowledge on the doorstep of every inner city school—these were among the objectives of the communal oral history and herstory campaign behind the production of the book of Sheffield herstories, *Lives of Love and Hope*. These lives of Sheffield mothers and grandmothers told to their daughters and sons—students at the local and ordinary Earl Marshal Comprehensive school in north-east Sheffield—were translated from at least five mother tongues, transcribed and edited by its students, and speak proudly of Pakistan and Somalia, Yemen, the Caribbean, Syria and Bangladesh as well as Sheffield and other places in South Yorkshire. They affirm the school's internationalism and that of its constituent communities, promote its antiracism and its function as a crucible of inter-cultural communication and understanding—and exemplify the importance given to 'story' as a vital form of critical literacy by Brazilian educator Paulo Freire: 'Narratives of liberation are always tied to people's stories and what stories we choose to tell and the way in which we decide to tell them, form the provisional basis of what a critical pedagogy of the future might mean.'

For in the hearts of our inner cities are classrooms of the world, and the world beats in our classrooms. The stories our students and their parents tell—be it of the flight from civil war in northern Somlia, the struggle against a forced marriage in a Bengal village, the life of a miner's family in a Yorkshire pit village, the blinding of a young husband in the anti-colonial war in Aden, a childhood idyll in rural Jamaica, a broken marriage in Pitsmoor, Sheffield or the endless labour of a wife's life on a farm in Kashmir—these are the world's stories, a part of a universal curriculum that finds identity and pride in being and telling about being a human in the world.

Such stories also act as sources and energies for emulation and as effective motivators for further study. For after women from so many places on the earth have told their stories and shown the unity of their experience of childcare, drudgery, enterprise, rebellion, migration, endless work and struggle—they also speak as one in their individual voices about the importance of education for those who come after—an education which they were mostly denied. 'You only live once so make the most of it,' declares a Pakistani mother, 'and get a good education, for that will open any good doors for you in the future.' 'Get as much education as you can!' insists a Sheffield mother, in tune with a Yemeni neighbour who says to her son, 'work hard, play hard and get the best out of your education'—while a Bangladeshi aunt concludes: 'Men should realise that women have their individuality and should learn to respect their lives and other women. We women need to change our attitude to life, otherwise men will continue to take advantage of us.'

In their self-assessments following the completion of these herstories and their publication in a 200 page book for the community—*Lives of Love and Hope* (the title is taken from a poem by Emteaz Hussain, a young Pakistani woman and ex-student of the school, who wrote

> And we were raised in the life of love and hope
> Because I was born the daughter of a steel-worker
> And the baby of a mother with the name of Asha
> And I was raised in the light and I was born to fight ...)

the students set down how the new knowledge of their mothers' lifetimes had meant new understanding and held much that they had never realised before. For many of them, their mothers' herstories were included as an example of factual writing in their GCSE evaluation folders, and they became an important factor in the three hundred per cent improvement in English examination results achieved by their year, compared to the year before. An enormous amount of effort had been put into these herstories. One Yemeni student had been waiting for his mother to arrive from the homeland before he could do his interview with her. Her passage was delayed, so in order to write his herstory he telephoned her in Sana'a and interviewed her over the wires, spending a great deal of a limited family budget to do so. Such was a measure of his motivation and commitment. A Bengali girl whose father's antipathy towards her studying made it extremely difficult for her to work at home, transcribed her herstory sitting in bed in a cold room in the early hours of the morning, which was the only time when she could work undisturbed and unprovoked. A Somali boy, having been in Britain for only two years, a refugee from civil war who had arrived in Sheffield directly from a camp in Ethiopia and who knew no English at all upon his arrival, achieved a 'C' pass at GCSE, notwithstanding the fact that a bout of tuberculosis had kept him away from school and his studies for two months during his examination course. These were some of the other stories behind the herstories.

All this demonstrated the impact of this form of curriculum process: democratic, participatory and community-orientated, emphasising Freire's point of 'what stories we choose to tell and the way in which we choose to tell them.' For these herstories, revealing the huge achievement and stamina within the development of their own families and communities and the potential of its creative application to the daughters and sons, also helped to boost achievement in the more conventional terms of examination and academic success—thus living out the school's watchwords: 'For excellence and community.' They also illustrated how, conversely to everything that the conservative restoration in education represents, the state must listen to the people, and allow them—alongside their teachers—to create a framework for their own education. For as Marx wrote prophetically over a century ago: 'the state has need of a very stern education by the people.'

This last point is crucial, for our communities must make their own curriculum priorities for the genuine benefit of their own people, young and adult, who are demanding more resources for education and the forging of new perspectives of knowledge which affirm their own past and guide them towards the future. For whose knowledge is it, whose version of history and language is it that is being imposed through the 'National Curriculum' in Britain and the similar affliction being planned by those in power in the USA.? Our communities, in projects like *Lives of Love and Hope*, are making pathways of curriculum and process around such life-affecting issues as racism, unemployment, attack on health and the environment, sexism, the social desperation that leads directly to increased crime and drug abuse, the contempt shown to the culture and languages that are seen as (even as I write this) un-British, with the Thatcherite and Churchillian contentions about 'halting the relentless flow of immigrants ... if we are to preserve the British way of life' to prevent the ungodly and unpatriotic spectacle of 'the muezzin calling Allah's faithful to the High Street mosque.'

The National Curriculum itself is a part of that same version of 'the British way of life'. As an integral part of the vast and backward market enterprise of the 1988 Education Reform Act, it is the reinforcer of these crude, narrow and racist propositions. Teachers and parents are now beginning to recognise that the whole structural entity of the Act from its creation of 'opted out' schools and the attempted destruction of comprehensive education principles to the pernicious and relentless testing, mass exclusions, the elitist 'City Technology Colleges' and the insistence on regular Christian assemblies and acts of worship—all this constitutes a smothering of the prospects of a democratic and community-based education that serves all our young people and their parents. Opposed to this convergent and regulated version of training and instruction—for it cannot be truly called education—is the development of a critical and life-opening form of education and literacy, where each new word (or old word) and number, signals a hope for greater understanding, choice and involvement in the betterment of community life and individual fulfilment. As Michael Apple has most eloquently put it: 'Critical literacy, powerful literacy, political literacy which enables the growth of genuine understanding and control of all the spheres of social life in which we participate.'

Such a curriculum and its active implementation is not an ideal: it is a practical aim, a real strategy. But it needs inner city schools to show the leadership of active resistance to the 'orders' of the National Curriculum, to go beyond their narrow confines. This means involving parents, teachers, students and whole communities—the people and the professionals, in a constant process of cooperatively building new curriculum projects and consolidating within the school new knowledge areas of language, history, culture and discourse. It will be a curriculum where campaigning is education, where knowledge also means how to fight to keep your school open, how to make it thrive with community use, how to out-manoeuvre the state agencies who want to tell these communities what their schools should teach and what their children should learn—and seek to rubber stamp 'Official Knowledge' on the hearts of inner cities and on the minds of their children. Instead, we must develop and present our own exemplars of liberation and achievement in education forged by ordinary people in their communities all over the world.

Notes

1   Apple, M, *Official Knowledge: Democratic Education in a Conservative Age*, Routledge, London and New York, 1993

2   Said, Edward W., *Culture and Imperialism*, Chatto and Windus, London, 1993

3   'See Milani, Farzaneh *Veils and Words*, I.B. Tauris, London 1993)

4   Searle, Chris (ed.) *Lives of Love and Hope: a Sheffield Herstory,* Earl Marshal School, Sheffield 1993.

5   From introduction by Paulo Freire in McLaren, Peter and Leonard, Peter (eds.), Pau*lo Freire: A critical encounter*, Routledge, London and New York, 1993; Paulo Freire: a Critical Encounter (Routledge, London and New York, 1993)

6   Marx, Karl, *Critique of the Gotha Programme*

7   Report of speech given by Winston Churchill MP, *The Guardian*, May 29 1993

8   Apple, Michael W., op. cit

Outcast England: School exclusion, racism and the failure of the Education Reform Act   (1994)

Perhaps the most shameful result of the 1988 Education Reform Act has been its effect of denying any education at all to growing numbers of British inner-city children.

We live in a county that once proudly talked about pioneering 'universal education'. This meant that *all* its children went to school, that school itself was compulsory and that those parents who wilfully kept their children away from school would be breaking the law. Yet now the education system, changed so fundamentally since the 1988 'reforms' have given it a completely new orientation, creates the conditions for many young people not to go to any school at all. So much so, that in a survey of pupils excluded permanently from school conducted recently by the Secondary Headteachers' Association, it was found that a quarter of such students simply vanished from the state education system that is legally obliged to educate them.[1] And we are referring to thousands of young people of school age, a large dispoportion of whom are from British black communities.

Disappearing pupils

This is how it happens. The Education Reform Act and the baggage of legislation that has followed it created a market system of education. The introduction of 'open enrolment' superseded the concept of defined catchment areas for each neighbourhood school. Thus schools are pressurised to compete for pupil heads. Examination league tables are becoming the means, supposedly, of defining the 'best' schools. Truancy tables, the public are being persuaded, are another barometer by which we select the most desirable schools for our children. So the temptation is becoming stronger and stronger for school managements to choose not to admit, or to permanently exclude those students who are thought to be disruptive, deemed 'difficult' to teach or who seem to offer only nuisance value. Or to take the least line of resistance that one Sheffield school has taken—solve your truancy problems and push yourself high up the ratings by expelling all your worst truants.

There is, of course, a grim irony in all of this. The Thatcher Government heralded the 1988 Act by announcing that it would, at last give parents the long-desired 'choice' of sending their children to whatever school they wished. The power of the local education authority to restrict this choice by the catchment area system would be swept away, with parents gaining new freedoms of choosing. What in fact has happened is that it is now the schools that are choosing the children with the 'desirable' schools in prosperous and suburban areas exercising their new freedom under the market to pick who they want and reject who they do not want—the latter usually finding their ways to the hard-pressed inner-city schools, with their higher level of pedagogical challenge and frequently lower level of resourcing.

Hoisted by their own petard, government ministers have realised that they have been trapped by the regressive consequences of their own legislation. In their so-called 'new framework- for schools' published in 1992, and titled (to the chagrin of millions of parents) *Choice and Diversity*, the Department for Education (DfE) authors declare, 'There are too many children playing truant. There are also too many children excluded from school, either temporarily or permanently.' There are, of course, no comments on how the irrelevance, boredom and lack of motivation induced by the prescription and narrowness of the National Curriculum may be making schools less interesting places. But as money can buy almost anything in the market the DfE announced in December 1992 that schools 'which took on unruly pupils might qualify for enhancements of their budgets' while schools which excluded pupils could be fined.[1]

The huge pressures facing many inner-city families, from high unemployment, poverty, bad housing, higher levels of serious illness and stress, the separation of parents, crime and racial harassment—all mean that inner-city children are more liable to bring their discontent, frustration and rebelliousness into school, and thus more likely to experience conflict or get into trouble there. If such problems become extreme or too complex for the school to handle—or cause behaviour that persistently interferes with other students' progress—what can be done?

The student can be 'statemented'. This is a long and detailed process of assessment of the special needs of the children and how they will be met by the local education authority (LEA). It takes an average of 15 months to complete and frequently takes much longer. It requires the involvement of an educational psychologist—often perceived as the 'gatekeeper' of the process—who, for the best of reasons for the readjustment of the student, may conclude that he or she should stay in the mainstream of the school where they presently attend, with a little extra support provided. The school, pleading that the student is too disruptive may not agree. Even if it is finally decided that the student is best helped by a place in a special school, this solution might take months to implement as a place may not be currently available. With LEAs receiving less and less money for children with 'special needs' and with the Major Government announcing through the Audit Commission Report, *Getting the Act Together,* that special schools should be phased out,' student placements in educationally supportive schools directed towards their particular needs are becoming more and more difficult to manage and the waiting periods becoming increasingly desperate for all concerned. Another factor is that a statemented student brings further expense to the LEA, which is legally bound to attach additional resources to that student. So some

LEAs in stringent financial circumstances have been reluctant to statement, realising that the outcome of the process will be an extra cost on their budget.

The result: children stay at home, betwixt and between, or wander the streets out of school while their case is being dealt with—for there are also fewer and fewer resources available for 'home tutoring'. 'Disruptive' students may finally (after an arduous and months-long process of persuasion and documentation by the mainstream school) be sent to a special school miles away from their homes. Then, because of the long bus journeys facing them every day, they may not attend at all. Such students, along with those who have been excluded from school with no prospect of alternative provision can then become as magnets to their friends still at school, who begin to truant in order to be with them. The interlocking problems of exclusion and truancy then become as one, as more and more truants and excluded students make for arcades, shopping malls or city centres, often to pursue other forms of learning in solvent abuse, shoplifting or car theft.

Exclusion, or expulsion?

There is much mystification surrounding the word 'exclusion' in education parlance. Schools do not refer to 'expulsions' now, even though almost all parents would know what that means. The preferred term is 'permanent exclusion', but it means the same thing. Other forms of exclusion, 'fixed term' or 'indefinite', are not expulsions and the student still remains a member of the school, with the school continuing to receive the budgetary allocation attached to the student while not having what it may see as the difficult duty of teaching him or her. But these are the official exclusions. The Warwick University researcher Margaret Stirling, who has done much pioneering work delving into this issue, concluded that in the LEAs where she conducted her inquires, 'unofficial exclusions may far outnumber those which are officially recorded and reported'.[6] Students have been, sent home from school without the correct procedures being observed and without the LEA knowing, or informal exclusions have become condoned truancies because the school has felt less pressurised when particular students have remained absent from lessons. Whatever the form of exclusion, what is clear is that excluded students ire far more likely to become involved in delinquent or criminal behaviour within the community of the school than students who remain at school and benefit from its more constructive and protected environment. They are also, of course, more likely to move towards solutions which will set them back on the path of useful and stimulating learning.

'Fixed-term' exclusions are used routinely by schools, sometimes as a sanction, but more often as a device to send students home in order to 'cool down' if they have been involved in fighting, racism, or threatening or seriously disruptive behaviour. The objective is usually to ensure that a parent comes up to school the next morning (or as soon as possible) so that the issue can be resolved with full parental consultation with the student recommencing his or her studies immediately. This system can work most effectively, except when the meeting with the parent becomes delayed and the student misses out on schooling with the continuity of study seriously disturbed.

'Indefinite' exclusions are much more damaging to the education of the student, there being no date set down by the school for his or her return to classes-although in such a case, the LEA is obliged to set one. Yet sometimes schools are pressurised to indefinitely exclude, in order to trigger a referral for special education for a student. Often, if a school is striving to secure a place in a special school that would clearly benefit a student, the school's chance of obtaining the place is much improved if the student is excluded. While he or she remains in mainstream education it is assumed by the LEA that the present arrangements are 'coping' and that the claim for a referral to a special school will not be considered a priority. Headteachers may sometimes be 'advised to exclude' certain students in order to hasten their chances to find places in special schools. Thus schools are placed in invidious situations of not wanting to exclude because of the disruption to a student's regular education however imperfect that may be—yet knowing that it is only through exclusion that the school can give the student the opportunity of the special resources that they need.

Sometimes such a course of action seems to be the only expedient. Take the case of Ahmed, a 13 year old boy recently arrived from Pakistan, who was having serious problems in learning English in his mainstream school. He was clearly in need of specialised English as a Second Language and learning difficulties support beyond that which the school was able to offer, and his teachers found that they could benefit him little in the mainstream context. His language learning was not progressing, he would become very quickly distressed and disruptive in classes, and he was eventually adjudged a safety risk both to himself and his classmates. Appeals to the LEA for him to be placed in a special school where he could get much closer and skilled attention were getting nowhere because of the squeeze on special education resources and because, as far as the 'system' was concerned, he was still in mainstream education and attending regularly, therefore it was 'coping' and other more serious priorities would have to come before his case.

Thus the only step a school can take in such a situation when it considers it absolutely essential for a student to have a special school place, is to try to *make* that student a priority by excluding him or her from the mainstream school and putting the responsibility for his special education back with the LEA. Such 'triggering' is fraught with risk because the underfunding and under-resourcing of LEAs by central government means that they are often constrained to move very slowly. In this case, Ahmed was indefinitely excluded with parental agreement but it took several months to get him regular home tuition and over a year for an assessment by an educational psychologist, Finally, after much internal campaigning and complaining by the school and the intervention by the local council for racial equality a place in a special school was secured for Ahmed. Such arrangements represent a system without a system, are powerfully discriminatory and damaging to young people's education and cannot be allowed to continue.

A culture of exclusion

In the LEA where I worked as a headteacher, there had been a significant rise in permanent exclusions which reflected a national trend. In 1988 in Sheffield, there were 48, by 1990 this had risen to 89. Other cities—Birmingham for example, showed a stark increase in the exclusions of much younger students of primary school age. And these are what Margaret Stirling calls the 'tip of the iceberg' exclusions—the ones that are recorded.

Such figures show that since the imposition of the 1988 Act across the country's schools, there has been a serious escalation of an 'exclusion culture' within them. Some schools have operated high profile exclusions as a part of their systems of discipline for many years: others have become notorious for their regular use of under-the-carpet exclusions. But the 1988 watershed has meant that instead of mainstream schools persevering, trying everything and relentlessly and untiringly seeking creative solutions for 'difficult' students, always insisting that they stay within the mainstream school and struggle for improvement—the massive workload now placed upon teachers of all the paraphernalia of the National Curriculum, means that schools move much more quickly, readily and prematurely towards permanent exclusion as a disciplinary measure. Teachers are frequently more exhausted, less patient, and with less time to devote to 'pastoral' or welfare issues, are genuinely much more strained. The introduction of new Child Protection procedures—often without any proper information or training—means that many teachers are having to switch from some of the old, authoritarian and more belligerent approaches to discipline to more acceptable models at the very period in their career when they are most under pressure. Thus the grasp of the exclusion measure can appear to offer relief from further classroom stress. Teacher reprimands backed up by statements like 'Any more of that and you'll be out of this school!' are becoming much more common, and unfortunately much more directly prophetic in schools.

In my own experience the growth of this 'exclusion' culture in schools is a relatively recent phenomenon. In the seventies in London, for example, permanent exclusions seemed to be very rare indeed. Teachers would often use their precious preparation time to go out-of school and round up truanting students from snooker halls or market stalls. The difference now is that such non-teaching time is a genuine luxury and rarity, and although teachers still do their best to attend to the pastoral and personal needs of their students they are much more ground down by central government curriculum rigmarole. The system gives every encouragement and incentive to exclude, by the way in which 'school success' is measured. Schools single-mindedly intent upon winning their way up the league tables are much more inclined to view 'difficult' students as unwanted ballast, and drop them. As the General Secretary of the National Association of Headteachers, David Hart, has asserted 'You are probably twenty times more likely to be excluded now than you were thirty years ago.'

The once-strong notion that local comprehensive schools should be expected to take *all children* of secondary school age from within a catchment area—those motivated and de-motivated, those academically inclined and those less so—is fast being eroded. 'Open enrolment' and larger and better-resourced schools picking and rejecting their students is contributing to creating a teenage underclass of turned aside, unschooled and outcast young people who are simply not going to school. As Margaret Stirling has acutely observed: 'Heads who had previously been sympathetic to offering extra support to difficult and underachieving pupils were now seeing them as a liability.'[7] It represents a tragic retreat from the principles of comprehensive education and it means that a rapidly-increasing minority of our school-age population are learning their Victorian values through the cut ad thrust of street life. Another survey carried out for the National Union of Teachers, Britain's largest teachers' union, reported in June 1992 that the number of excluded students may have risen by 20 per cent during the previous year. 'Schools expel more bad apples', headlined the *Guardian* asserting that schools were excluding troublesome students in order to 'improve their image', fearing 'that disruptive children would drag down their reputations when they were required to publish examination league tables.'[8] Doug McAvoy, NUT General Secretary, was quoted as saying: 'The findings show that pressure on school resources has made it increasingly difficult to respond to the needs of children with behavioural problems.'

School exclusion and racism

Over twenty years ago the Caribbean community in London and other British cities waged a very successful campaign in highlighting the disproportionate numbers of their children being sent to schools for the so-called 'educationally sub-normal'. A famous pamphlet authored by a black London teacher named Bernard Coard was published called *How the West Indian child is made educationally sub-normal in the British school system*.[9] This had a profound influence and helped to develop progressive changes in Special Education during the years that followed—including the demise of 'ESN' schools themselves. Another important campaign was organised during the mid eighties around the issue of exclusions (then called 'suspensions'). Reports from secondary schools in Nottingham, Reading, Bristol and the north London Borough of Brent showed that black students were up to six times more likely to be suspended from school than their white peers.'[10] The *Times Educational Supplement*,[11] quoting from a Commission for Racial Equality survey, reported that in Birmingham, England's second city, black students were four times more likely to be suspended, and the *Sheffield Star*[12] revealed that a council probe had been launched—following a black community campaign—in order to determine 'details of all black children expelled, suspended and referred to special schools since 1980 in an attempt to find out how many children are affected.' The Ukaidi Community Link Project, a black people's organisation in Nottingham, produced their own pamphlet, *Suspensions and the Black Child,*[13] which offered powerful evidence into the disproportionate percentages of black student exclusion as well as repeated instances of teacher racism and the use of belligerent and provocative forms of discipline.

Thus there is a well-established tradition of black community resistance to the inequitable use of exclusion against black school students, a tradition which will no doubt be continually invoked while the present situation persists. For among the statistics about school exclusions nationally, introduced by the junior education Minister Eric Forth in December 1992—which included a figure of 3000, 87 per cent of whom were in secondary schools and with boys four times more likely to be excluded than girls—was the disproportionate representation of black students, 8.1 per cent of the total figure from only 2 per cent of the national school population.

Recent documentation of a more local nature tells a similar racist tale. In Sheffield in 1990, even though African-Caribbean children only composed 2 per cent of the school population, 6.7 per cent of excluded children were African-Caribbean. The situation in Birmingham is still very bad: 9 per cent of the school population African-Caribbean, yet they accounted for 31 per cent of the exclusions. In Nottingham schools, if you are African-Caribbean you have five times more likelihood of being excluded than a white child. In Lewisham, south London, 61 per cent of exclusions were African-Caribbean, even though only 14 per cent were from that community.

The politicians, officers and teachers of the British state education system have proffered many reasons for such statistics over the years. In Nottingham in 1985, Caribbean parents were campaigning also against the comments made by a local councillor who declared that black children were suspended more than white children because there was a 'high proportion of single-parent black families in the black community.'[15] During the same year, the National Association of Schoolmasters and Union of Women Teachers (NASUWT) argued in their pamphlet, *Multi-ethnic Education,* that it was 'singularly unhelpful' to argue that 'inherent racism in teachers' was a primary reason for the continuing bad experiences many black children have within the British school systems although, they conceded, 'some teachers may have formed stereotyped ideas of West Indian children and their abilities.'[16] Rather, they continued, 'it is *external* factors and relationships which has a strong bearing on whether or not children from different minority groups perform well at school.' The authors— their views apparently representing those of Britain's second-largest teachers' union— then proceed to construct arguments about black students and their communities that are stricken with ignorance and cultural insult.

'For example, Asian children, unlike West Indian, are largely the products of a stable cultural background, enjoying the benefit of their own language, religions and values which place great emphasis on the need for learning as a means of self improvement and a solid foundation for success in life.' The child has an identifiable and secure sense of its own ethnic identity within one (sic) of the great cultures of civilisation.

In contrast, many West Indian children suffer from the fact that they belong to a sub-culture of British culture with no readily identifiable distinctiveness.'

From here, where?

The ignorance of teachers and the school system generally about the communities whom they serve is still a vital factor which promotes conflict and misunderstanding between teachers and students. It also hardens alienation and means that schools and communities often still find it difficult to really know and trust each other. Excessive exclusions and the provocative school culture which breeds them are still often a result of this unease and ignorance. Our schools need to be ever less arrogant, more receptive, more ready to learn from their communities—and less eager to assume that they have a monopoly of knowledge and experience to impart and implant, an attitude, of course, reinforced by the one-way education of the National Curriculum. Schools need to trust their communities more with the use of their precious educational resources in evenings and at weekends opening them up to community use and progress in supplementary classes, language schools and genuinely community-controlled education projects.

Schools have a responsibility to make their codes of discipline and accepted conduct clear, setting them down unambiguously. These must include exclusions procedures, offering guidelines to parents for consultations, advice and independent appeals. For a school to take a 'reforming' attitude towards exclusions by limiting them and seeking to end them by developing the institutional culture and effective disciplinary means to resolve conflict and disruption internally without resorting to methods of exclusion— is a difficult and challenging step. If a headteacher begins to change the school's disciplinary system away from a reliance upon exclusion, she is likely to find instant enemies among teachers within the school who have depended upon the exclusion expedient for years and years. Likewise, if a progressive section of teachers sets out to change the system from below, they can easily be blocked by more senior teachers or a school management that would prefer things to stay as they are. Schools, of course, can be inordinately conservative places that are both nervous and hostile to the face of change—particularly where long-established structures of discipline are involved. Yet this process of change must happen and communities and governing bodies may need to oversee it to happen, with teachers themselves looking even harder to forge more creative and successful *internal* solutions to the ever-live problems of school discipline.

Yet centrally it is very difficult to see prospects of widespread change on the issue of school exclusions as with all the associated abuses in the British school system, unless parents, teachers, students and communities adopt a more coherent and nationally networked campaigning approach against Government education policy and the effects of the 1988 Act. There will be no improvement for example, or availability in special education resources, unless the threatened demise of LEAs is prevented by public pressure and more resources and finances are returned to them by Government for local provision. Thus defence of LEAs is an essential area of public activity. The National Curriculum, with its gradgrindian sequence of learning and testing, the narrow cultural chauvinism of its approach to knowledge and human experience and its blatantly racist exclusion of the cultures, histories, languages and perspectives of Britain's black people, is already creating a tedium and uniformity of school curriculum which will do nothing to spark the interest and motivation of young people to learn. Similarly, parents will need more and more to defend their children's schools from any moves towards 'opting out' of LEA funding and from adopting Grant Maintained status. This will only take more precious resources from other local schools and create even more divisiveness and market competition in the system. And 'open enrolment' threatens to close down remaining educational resources in working class neighbourhoods, creating even larger, better-resourced and privileged schools in more affluent suburbs with long distance education, busing and far-away schools, the outcome for thousands of working class and black children through the cities of Britain.

All these facets of Conservative education legislation are a part of the same single regressive enterprise, and need to be countered at all points and ends of the system.

Yet the 'exclusions' issue shows us one of the sharpest and clearest deformities of the system, and one which affects thousands of young people and their parents on a daily basis, cutting them off from their human right and entitlement to the best in education. A 'plague bacillus which will infect its community',[17] was how John Sutton, General Secretary of the Secondary Heads' Association, described the excluded student who is seeking admission to an alternative school. The barbarism of the Act is also expressed in such concepts and attitudes a part of the mentality of exclusion. And walk around the luxurious and shining new shopping centres of Britain, or around our inner-cities. If you believe in universal state education you may feel a sense of deep shame. Be ready to count the number of school-age children that you see, missing the most valuable social process that a child needs and is a child's right. Then go and read a book like Gilberto Dimenstein's nightmarish *Brazil: War on Children*,[18] which profiles the lives and experiences of danger, crime, disease and death of the children of Brazilian cities to whom school is an irrelevance because they have been constantly, all their lives, rejected by it—and have then, as a consequence sought to reject it themselves. A dialectic of despair and socialised ignorance, but you would be reading about how things could develop in Britain unless schools, communities and local education authorities combine to use every energy to bring back the outcast children of our own times—who have so much creative strength and potential boiling inside them. In being determined to do this, we would also be rejecting the backward dogma of the educational market place that has already made these precious children its soiled and unsaleable goods.

Notes

1   Stirling, Margaret, How many pupils are being excluded?, in
    British Journal of Special Education, Vol. 19 No. 4,1992.
2   *Choice and Diversity. A New Framework for Schools,* Department for Education, London, 1992
3   *Independent,* 1 December, 1992
4   *Guardian,* 30 June 1992
5   *Morning Star,* 5 November, 1992
6   op cit
7   Ibid.
8   *Guardian,* 17 June 1992
9   Coard, Bernard, *How the West Indian child is made educationally sub-normal in the British school system,* New Beacon Books, 1970 (Reprinted by Karia Press 1991).
10 *Caribbean Times,* 8 March 1985
11 *Times Educational Supplement,* 12 April 1985
12 *Sheffield Star,* 22 March 1985
13 *Suspensions and the Black Child,* Ukaidi Community Link Projects, Nottingham 1984.
14 *Guardian,* December, 1992
15 *Caribbean Times,* 8 March 1985
16 *Multi-ethnic Education,* National Association of Schoolmasters/Union of Women Teachers. London, 1985
17 *Education,* September, 1991
18 Dimenstein, Gilberto, *Brazil: War on Children,* Latin America Bureau, 1992

'OFSTEDED, BLUNKETTED AND PERMANENTLY EXCLUDED'
(1996)

There is no question that equitable and effective mechanisms of external monitoring and inspection are essential in any legitimate system of schooling. Through such ways are its values, quality and efficiency determined. The point at issue in this story, however, is whether this particular state school inspection agency, OFSTED (the Office for Standards in Education), established as part and parcel of the equipage following the 1988 Education Reform Act of the Margaret Thatcher government, does or can serve that imperative.

The integrity of an authentic inspectorate does not lie in the role of policing what is, in effect, an exclusive, monocultural, government determined 'National Curriculum'. Rather, it needs to be critically alive to how such a narrow concept of the curriculum can actually suppress dynamic knowledge or the shared process of learning by both students and teachers in classrooms. This is so particularly within the cosmopolitan context of many British inner-city schools where internationalism overrides things 'national', multilingualism goes beyond learning in a single language, and breadth of experience and understanding across many cultures eclipse a parochial consciousness or one forged by the limitations of knowing but one place, one frame of reference and one dimension of living. 'And what do they know of England, who only England know?'

As the hegemony of the 'National Curriculum' has been incrementally institutionalised throughout British state schools, the OFSTED formula for inspection has been established to match its uniformity.

This formula was devised to be applied to 'mainstream' suburban schools with predominantly white and middle-class school populations, serving constituencies largely favourable to the Conservative Party and comprised mainly of its voters. It may seem to be appropriate to the interests of a monocultural, mono-faith, monolingual and decidedly white ethos. It certainly does not include a set of criteria apposite to an inner-city, multiracial and multilingual community, where the lives of people are potentially broader, more attuned to struggle and adaptation, and where vision stretches beyond the local, national, white and European. A National Curriculum which is confined to a state-licensed body of knowledge, processes and perspectives across approved subject areas, serves only to limit that potential, blunt that vision.

Moreover, OFSTED is cast in the role of both judge and jury. Through its public judgments and pronouncements based on limited and formulaic criteria, it can become the executioner of schools as well as the constable of the curriculum that those same schools are compelled to 'deliver'. Those most at risk from OFSTED interventions are those whose *raison d'etre* is not, and cannot be, contained within the narrow tram-lined criteria and the limited curriculum which OFSTED was founded to patrol and guard. Thus, when we read of particular OFSTED offensives in identified inner-city areas and how such areas—with their networks of black education officers, local politicians, concerned teachers, governors and parents—are being targeted for concentrated inspection, it only confirms this judgment. In October 1995, the inspectorate announced a 'blitz' of inspections to cover the mainly inner-city London boroughs of Lambeth (seventy four schools) and Waltham Forest (sixty schools).[1] Coming as it did on the eve of the Conservative Party conference in Blackpool, the move was termed by opposition education spokesman David Blunkett 'political'. But this was only the most recent example of such an inequitable focus. In July 1994, Elaine Foster, headteacher of the predominantly black Handsworth Wood School in Birmingham, told the *Times Educational Supplement*: 'I know eight or nine black heads and six of us were inspected in the first round of inspection. Some of my colleagues have been totally devastated by the experience.' Ms Foster also spoke of the lack of black and bilingual inspectors to inspect schools with large percentages of black children and how the very few black OFSTED inspectors had been 'systematically marginalised' during the course of the inspection process.[2]

In its report *Access and Achievement in Urban Education*, published in 1993, OFSTED declared: 'Most schools in these disadvantaged areas do not have within themselves the capacity for sustaining renewal. The rising tide of national educational change is not lifting these boats.'[3] Therein lies the myth of OFSTED and the lies it fosters. For 'the rising tide of national educational change' is more of a quicksand in which ever greater numbers of schools, teachers and pupils are becoming mired. What is actually being articulated is a deficit vision of inner-city schools and their communities at odds with a process of change. But such change is, in fact, regressive and hostile to their interests. It cannot sustain them because it runs contrary to their strengths and potential. It is, in contradiction, by using the dynamism of schools in the inner city and the communities which they serve that solutions and genuine achievement can be nurtured. The source of the problem lies not within individual schools so much as in their inadequate resourcing, the stringency of their budgets and the uniform and often times alien curriculum which they are compelled to 'deliver'. This demotivates students, uses teachers uncreatively (as servers of pre-cooked knowledge, rather than participants in a shared educational process) and demeans the communities that the schools serve by ignoring and excluding their wealth of knowledge, internationalism and culture. Inner-city schools do, indeed, have it within themselves and their communities to develop and be transformed by their own creative energies and are anything but beached vessels. Remembering the words of Tom Paine, they 'have it in themselves to make their world new again', and would do so with much greater facility if they did not have the incubus of an imposed curriculum, a backward Education Act and a tendentious inspectorial system weighing them down.

The inspectors call

When OFSTED inspected Earl Marshal Comprehensive School in north-cast Sheffield (where the author was, at the time, the headteacher) in two separate exercises in May and July 1995 which were later fused into one unitary inspection, its judgments could be placed into two categories.[4] There were the often perceptive and helpful criticisms on professional matters: the quality of teaching and learning, of internal systems and management at all levels within the school, of organisation inside and outside of the classroom. These were tough and many of them were true criticisms which the school needed to internalise, consider, take as its own and adopt self-critically.

These were legitimate professional insights, most of which the school accepted and resolved to move upon and create the necessary improvements. But there were also issues raised that were in another category—in reality, attacks that stretched beyond the professional. For criticism enters another dimension entirely when a team of OFSTED inspectors (with very little experience of inner-city schools and with only one black member who is not, anyway, an inspector) devalues a school's ethos because it seeks to affirm the experience, history, languages and faiths of its constituents. Over 80 per cent of Earl Marshal's students are from black, arrivant families from countries once colonised by Britain—from Pakistan, Somalia, Yemen and the Caribbean, and where, for the main part, religions other than Christianity were dominant. And yet the school's ethos was described as having a 'lack of balance', with insufficient emphasis upon European civilisation. It took a long discussion after the draft of the report was first read to the governors to persuade the team of authors not to use their original expression, 'neo-marxist', to describe the school's campaigning approach to education within its community. Yet would such a team condemn a school in a middle-class suburb or describe it as 'neo-bourgeois' for affirming the typical life and experience of the parents who send their children to it?

In Earl Marshal's case, very little positive was included about the school's huge investment in its community; that it has the largest Arabic supplementary school in the country operating from its buildings twice every weekend (organised, staffed and stewarded by the local Yemeni Community Association), that the Pakistani and Somali communities run their own classes there, or that the school supports the North's most successful and innovative cricket centre[6] and school-based community publishing project.[7] Such extracurricular pastoral work and strengthening of literacy and other skills could be seen as a foundation for more mainstream schooling. Instead, the school was condemned for its lowly place on GCSE league tables during the year of the inspection, despite having achieved a very significant improvement in these examinations the year before. Little acknowledgement was made of the successes the school has had in educating refugee children from Somalia and Yemen, their founding progress in learning English at the school and their subsequent achievements as 'late developers' after they have left school to enter further and higher education.

As the comprehensive school serving Sheffield's most economically disadvantaged area, Earl Marshal receives some extra 'positive action' funding. By careful budgeting and understanding that the school could face hard times ahead, it had built up an underspend during the years before the inspection, anticipating cuts in funding and the consequent threats to teachers' jobs. When the school decided to allocate this underspend to conserve the posts of specialist teachers and keep class sizes down to help directly its large majority of second-language learners and below-age readers, its management and governors were severely criticised by OFSTED for bad financial management and, in the price-conscious, value-ignorant jargon of the day, 'poor value for money'. This was in a context where Earl Marshal had saved the local education authority (LEA) many thousands of pounds every year by pursuing inclusive policies and not expelling students or sending them back to the LEA for high-cost special provision. Mainstream provision per pupil per year is around £2,000; special provision can cost up to £17,000. No credit was given to the school by OFSTED for this.

Instead, the recommendation in its report was that the school should 'urgently address the issues of a staffing model and responsibility structure related to the school's stated organisational, pastoral and curricular needs', which, broadly translated, meant that it should rationalise, reduce spending and shed teachers. Behind such recommendations, of course, lay the power to remove management and governing body, bring in 'educational associations' to run the school or, finally, to close it down. Thus recommendations take on the form of ultimatums, and this was what the school was receiving, over issues which went well beyond the pedagogic and professional, the rightful areas of inspectorial interest and influence. In fact, OFSTED was insisting, in its own coded terms, that the school had to change its strongly community-oriented ethos and also make a substantial part of its teaching staff redundant. This was not simply a routine exercise of school inspection or evaluation. It was the educational equivalent of a structural adjustment package, the like of which has, at the behest of the IMF and World Bank, condemned the children of Third World countries to inferior and substandard education. Here, the afflicted inner-city school (with the great majority of its students of Third World origin) has been forced into the role of the 'peripheral' nation striving to pursue a progressive path, with OFSTED acting out the part of the World Bank or the IMF.

These are new and dangerously subjective areas for inspectorial activity, reinforcing the political objectives of government, rather than the educational and professional responsibilities of criticising and developing schools for the benefit of their students and communities. They show how much power OFSTED has arrogated to itself at the behest of a government determined to push through its 1988 'reforms' as well as to 'downsize' the national teaching force. The overt political role of OFSTED becomes even clearer when the area of school governance is considered.[8]

The governors

Earl Marshal's governing body had the strongest black profile of any in Sheffield. At the time of the OFSTED interventions, more than half of its members were from local black communities and among them there was a strong professional element. The chair, a pioneer of the Yemeni Community Association, was the head of the city's community liaison teacher service and had been a school governor for over a decade. Such experience was simply waved away, one local OFSTED inspector describing him as 'not having a clue' about matters of school governance. The previous chair, still a governor, was the former director of Sheffield city council's first Race Equality Unit. Another member was the headteacher of a special school, another the deputy head of an inner-city primary school. Thus there was deep and broad professional expertise and community representation among the governors.

As on most governing bodies, there were some relatively inactive governors and some who, although committed in other ways to the life of the school, found meetings difficult to attend because of evening or night work driving taxis or engagement on the night shift of local steelworks. But the commitment of the active elements was continuous and exemplary, from the loyal support they had given in 1991 when the school needed to campaign hard to fight off a closure proposal by the LEA, to more recent times when they had helped organise temporary work experience placements and counselling in community centres for disaffected students as an effective alternative to school exclusion. They had made some excellent appointments of new teachers and substantially increased the proportion of black staff at the school. For the school's black intake had increased steadily over the previous five years, so that by December 1995 over 80 per cent its 550 students were from black communities. The number of black staff had increased from four in 1990 to twenty one in 1995, including a Head of Year and four heads or acting heads of department. And whereas there were two black governors in 1990, by 1995 there were eleven, including a black chair and representatives from all the school's constituent communities, forming a majority. The governors had also given invaluable help to the school in using their influence and physical presence to help curb the anti-social and sometimes violent activities of alienated youths around the school campus during the evenings. Such involvement had a substantial impact in keeping children away from delinquent activities and, incidentally, sparing the wider community from the costs of such behaviour. In short, their involvement had been cooperative and successful in standing up for the school and fighting for its survival and development.

But they were not school governors with the same life-style and habits as the suburban professionals who populated the governing bodies of schools in predominantly middle-class areas. They had not become governors because of a sole concern for their own individual children. Their governance is an extension of the struggles of their own inner-city communities. What motivates them is the development of their whole communities and the betterment of life for all the families in their part of the city through local state education. OFSTED did not approve of them and treated them with almost as much contempt as they did the headteacher, whose view of a head's role as a 'teacher with extended responsibilities'—in no way accorded with the new management culture being imposed upon schools, rejection of which is now, apparently, deemed akin to apostasy. As for the governors, their function was not to concern themselves with community development, mobilising local support and educational activity around the school, or stimulating a participatory process between teacher and pupil in a close and trusting relationship, but to confine themselves to detailed monitoring of school management, finance and curriculum, and to ensuring that the school restricted itself to the 'statutory requirements' of the National Curriculum and the 1988 Act. In short, each governing body is to become its own OFSTED, its own mini-inspectorate, even to the extent of fostering all the anxieties of a redundancy culture among teachers. Such an imposition on the governance of schools should concern every inner-city community which is struggling to achieve more control over its own local education resources and, in particular, its secondary schools. As such it represents a growing threat to local educational democracy, already bruised and curtailed.

Blunkett and the NASUWT

What were the forces which provoked these OFSTED interventions? In February 1994, David Blunkett, New Labour's shadow secretary of state for education, sent a letter to the director of education of Sheffield Education Department, requesting that I be 'removed' from my post as headteacher of Earl Marshal School. Despite requests from the chair of governors, members of the local Labour Party and my union the National Union of Teachers (NUT), to both Blunkett and the Education Department, I was never given a copy of this letter, although a concerned officer of the LEA showed it to me and allowed me to read it shortly after it arrived.

The letter described complaints received by Blunkett from a supply teacher who had spent less than two days at the school and from a 'teachers' association' subsequently established as the National Association of Schoolmasters/Union of Women Teachers (NASUWT). The background to NASUWT's involvement is significant. The school's inclusive policies had been a bone of contention to NASUWT members at the school for some time. They had been in dispute with me, as headteacher, over my refusal to permanently exclude certain students. They had embarked upon a strategy of refusing to teach these students in an attempt to force the adoption of a more frequent practice of permanent exclusion. This had been rejected both by myself and the governors. Blunkett's letter recommended that the director should call a meeting with the school governors (later a meeting of just Labour Party governors with Blunkett and the LEA was convened) to discuss my removal as headteacher.

This NASUWT action was consistent with the position of their general secretary Nigel De Gruchy, who was reported at the time as declaring that 'disruptive pupils were the biggest barrier to raising standards in schools'. In April, 1996 NASUWT members, this time at Glaisdale School, Nottingham, again threatened strike action if expelled student Richard Wilding, who had won an appeal to return to the school, was allowed back.[9] In October, 1996 NASUWT members shut Manton Junior School in Worksop after a ten-year-old boy was allowed back into school after winning an appeal.

I was not officially informed of the receipt of this letter and neither were the governors. Blunkett had not visited the school and never brought up the matters in his letter with myself as headteacher or the governors. He had heard of the school's internal workings primarily through a teacher who was hostile to the policies of the head and governors and through the letters sent by members and officers of the NASUWT.

It is worth noting the cordiality of the relationship between the shadow education secretary and the NASUWT by the time of the association's annual conference in April 1995. As the *Times Educational Supplement* recorded: 'The warmth of his reception was rapturous. It prompted Mr. Blunkett to remark, 'You are such a wonderful audience. And you are listening!'[10] This was far from the much more critical reaction to Blunkett when he had visited the traditionally more progressive NUT conference the week before. Here he found many teachers angry at the regressively right-wing drift of New Labour's educational policies, in particular the leader's embrace of grant-maintained schools, the threats to dismiss so-called 'weak' teachers and the excoriation of those teachers who were prepared to take strike action for greater resources and principled educational reasons.

As frequently happens within the closely-knit teacher culture of Sheffield, news of this letter was soon leaked to the local press, this time under the headline, 'Teacher bashing school defended by headteacher', with Blunkett's own comment as 'I think other people for their own reasons—are blowing up something which I've not communicated publicly'.[11] But for a public influential political figure to interfere privately and directly in the internal operations of an LEA and ask for the removal of a local headteacher was seen by many, particularly the NUT, to set a dangerous precedent. In their protests and attempts to secure natural justice, private citizens, community leaders, and union officials were certainly not exaggerating a real threat for all schools and teachers.

As well as David Blunkett, word also reached Her Majesty's Inspectorate in London which, along with OFSTED, began to show a particular interest in the school. With the LEA under pressure from both Blunkett and OFSTED to make a move on the school, its governors had little option but to pre-empt the inevitable and invite the local OFSTED team to conduct a full investigation of the school. This OFSTED did with a singular promptness. It was followed shortly after by a further inspection, negotiated by the LEA, carried out by a combined team of national and local inspectors. Thus the school received two OFSTED inspections within two months. Earl Marshal was labelled 'a failing school' after the second inspection and put in the category of schools requiring 'special measures'. This could be followed by the loss of delegated powers and a take-over of the school by an 'educational association' composed of external industrial managers and retired headteachers to replace the existing headteacher and governors. It was also compelled to send copies of both OFSTED reports (only a two-month interval between them) to the press and local radio. This adverse, repeated, high profile coverage caused dire reductions to the school's year 7 intake, a fall in roll and hence severe cuts to its pupil-generated budget. Thus, teachers' jobs were put at risk and the very future of the school threatened as a consequence of OFSTED's self-fulfilling predictions.

'Special measures'

The next term began in September 1995 with the school being given 'support' from the LEA through 'special measures'. This support consisted of regular visits by two local inspectors who had been part of the first inspection. They acted as a shadow senior management, spending much of their time in the school in efforts to reconstruct the head and deputy head into their conception of effective school managers. Sometimes these sessions became almost like interrogations, particularly around the school's commitment to an internationalism that went beyond the National Curriculum, and its priority of seeking to work with local communities through its governors, rather than treating the governors as separate controlling and monitoring agents, as required by OFSTED. The inspectors also systematically interviewed all members of the teaching staff and organised a training session on lesson planning by members of the LEA Quality Assurance Service. They did not visit classrooms or involve themselves with the day-to-day pedagogy of the school. Meanwhile, the head and deputy head began to put into effect the action plan devised by the governors as required by the second OFSTED inspection. The governors, meanwhile, were engaged in identifying potential redundancies within a strict deadline, in order to 'downsize' staffing — 3.5 teachers had to go by April, with the likelihood of four more being made redundant by September 1996. This was the first occasion during my headship that redundancies had had to be made.

As progress was being sustained in both these areas, the school was rocked by the sudden death, in late November, of the deputy head, whose deep human and professional commitment had been at the centre of school life and leadership. Thus the school was still in shock and grief when, less than a month later, on the last day of term, the LEA removed both the delegated powers of the governors and the headteacher at one stroke, even though the head had already agreed to take voluntary early retirement from May

1996. The formulator of a policy against the permanent exclusion of students found himself permanently excluded as headteacher. These measures came after the national OFSTED had informed the LEA that it had not given sufficient support to the school following the inspection and the drafting of the action plan. The drastic nature of the LEA's response to OFSTED's criticism could be interpreted as a device to deflect such criticisms away from the LEA and on to the governors and the head. The draconian nature of the LEA action was matched by the crassness of its timing, and was described by the head as having 'no moral legitimacy'.[12] But, from the LEA's perspective, it made sense to get a free run, without governor control, to appoint a new headteacher and deputy head more in line with its own ideology, and to hasten the redundancy process now that it had power over both school budget and appointment processes.

Unsurprisingly, the first 'public' figure to comment in the national media upon the LEA's move was Blunkett, who was quoted in the *Daily Telegraph* as 'welcoming' the action." Thus the process of 'removal' of the headteacher had come full circle. For three abiding fears lay behind the LEA's final action, apart from anxiety that the government might remove its powers and impose an 'educational association' to take control of the school. The first concerned the long campaign that had been built up by the NASUWT against the inclusive policies of the head and governors, in which permanent exclusion of a student was not to be carried out except in the most unresolvable of circumstances. Only one student was permanently excluded during a period of over five years—in a school which headed the LEA index of disadvantage by eight full points. The LEA, instead of supporting and standing up for this policy, which saved dozens of students over the years from a life on the streets and the LEA thousands of pounds in expensive school provision, succumbed to its detractors and buckled under the pressure from the NASUWT and its ally-in-chief. The second fear arose from the discomfiture of the LEA with the school's internationalism and, following from that, its questioning approach to the concept of the National Curriculum. The draft report of the first inspection (carried out by the LEA inspectorate) had expressed its concern about a 'lack of political balance' in the school, caricaturing as 'neo-Marxist' its critical view of British imperial history and the alternative perspectives expressed through the posters (such as those of the '*Whose World is the World?*' series) and the multilingual banners hanging in the school. Many of these had, in fact, been made during the campaign in 1991 to stop the school's closure by the same LEA. OFSTED had shown little interest in non-European views of world history and had criticised the schools 'bias' against European and British perspectives on history and 'civilisation'. When the headteacher put to one of the inspectors with an interest in the history syllabus that the perspectives of Caribbean historians such as Walter Rodney were also important guides to the teaching of the subject, the inspector replied that he had neither read nor heard of his work. A subsequent discussion between inspectors and officers at the LEA focused on what were referred to as the 'obscene' posters on the walls of the head's office. These included a photograph of some Mozambican women learning under the trees, above the slogan (translated from Portuguese) 'Let us make the entire country into a school where everyone learns and everyone teaches'; a poster from the Grenada literacy campaign with the words 'Each one teach one, let us learn together', and a Nicaraguan scene of some literacy teachers in a village under a volcano, with the slogan (from the Spanish), 'it is the duty of a person to be where they are most useful'.

Finally, and most significantly, the LEA feared the independence of the school's multiracial governing body, with its strong black leadership, This, containing some of the most professionally experienced, dedicated and intellectually able governors in the city, was expressly committed to community intervention and to exercising the power of local black and working-class people over curriculum policy, teacher appointments and overall school development within a cooperative relationship with the LEA. That such a governing body should seek to reduce the power of white LEA officials and paternalistic bureaucrats was not to be tolerated, despite the galaxy of official rhetoric about 'equal opportunities', 'community education' and 'anti-racist policies'.

The governors fight back

The governors, led by the black members, wasted no time in beginning a campaign against the LEA action. Given that the constitutional coup against the head and the governors was carried out the day before the Christmas break and during a time of mourning in the school for the late deputy head, it was greeted locally by little beyond perplexity and opprobrium. Here was a Labour LEA using recent and discredited Tory education law (the 1993 Education Act) to take away the legal rights of a representative and highly professional governing body that had had the boldness to challenge it, The government shibboleth of 'parental choice' and intervention had, on this occasion, been invoked by a predominantly black governing body but, as the *Asian Times* concluded in its editorial columns, the Earl Marshal events 'highlight the limits to parental choice, in cases where those parents are not white and middle class'.[14]

The chair of governors, Abdul Shalf, declared their intention not to be bulldozed by the LEA. As he said to the *Sheffield Star*: 'This is the only black-led governing body in the city, and we have been branded incapable. We are determined to defend ourselves.'[15]

The governors made four immediate demands of the LEA, threatening resignation and withdrawal of community support for the school should the LEA refuse to meet them. They insisted upon a timescale for the full restoration of the delegated powers; a report of the process leading up to the removal of powers, with copies of the complete correspondence relating to the school between the Department for Education and Employment (DfEE) and the LEA—much of which had been kept confidential; full involvement in the appointment of the new head and a public acknowledgement of the outgoing head's 'contribution to the school and its community'—the 'restoration of his integrity'. Thus the LEA was put under strong pressure as the media coverage of the governors' riposte, both locally and in the educational press, was widespread and sympathetic. Students at the school also seized the moment to demonstrate, boycotting classes and issuing leaflets in support of the ex-head.[16] They also expressed their disgust at the lies told to them that Searle had gone voluntarily—recalling the warning in Yevtushenko's poem:

> Telling lies to the young is wrong ...
> The young know what you mean. The young are people.[17]

Meanwhile, the governors issued a strong press statement making their position very clear. They accused the LEA of 'reckless and damaging action', and continued:

> We were particularly disappointed that the Authority was content to play into the current Government's philosophy of judging schools through the distorting mirror of league tables rather than looking at the situation of the children as they come into the school and the progress they make during their time at the school.
>
> For instance at Year 7 when children arrived at the school, the majority had a reading age well below their biological age, and had English as their second language. A substantial minority were children who are refugees and who had little or no experience of formal education and had no spoken or written English.
>
> To deliver a national curriculum to these children without attending to their immediate educational and social needs would be like feeding a starving child on unboned kippers.
>
> The Authority is well aware, for instance, of the school's policy on exclusion, and how this position was frequently undermined and challenged at every opportunity by a certain faction within the staff. At a time when there are nearly 200 young people excluded from Sheffield schools, we could be forgiven for expecting acknowledgement and appreciation of our efforts to find a better way to respond to this challenging situation.
>
> It is our contention that, at times, the actions of some of his [the head's] colleagues were nothing short of sabotage. The actions of a small faction within the staff were taken from the start of his appointment and continued up to recent times, and were even pursued by ex-members of staff. Again, the Authority is aware of an experience of English education our concern at the way in which these were given credence by senior officers of the Education Department.
>
> For some time now, Black communities in Sheffield have been aware that their issues are being swamped by the main policy changes that have taken place in schools. The situation is not unique to Sheffield, it is experienced nationally. One very damaging effect of the decentralising of education management has been an overall weakening in accountability and control over policy, practice and the procedures of decision-making. At Earl Marshal,

we were beginning to re-establish a sense of regaining some of that accountability and of the Community itself exercising some control. The actions taken by the Authority at Earl Marshal ride roughshod over our efforts and leave us feeling ever more certain that the Authority's erstwhile commitment to Racial Equality and Social Justice was nothing more than a fashionable flirtation.

Certainly, the LEA had a record of limiting and hampering the efforts of black Sheffielders when they sought to exercise power within the city's education system. The marginalisation of black officers from the mainstream affairs and structures of the LEA, the passing over of qualified and competent black professionals for promotions to senior positions and headships; the 'keeping out' and discouragement shown to black race equality officers and the shameful suggestions and innuendoes made against black professionals within the LEA—leading in one case to a colleague (who held a first and higher degree from Sheffield universities) having his qualifications secretly investigated by council officials years after he had been appointed. The action against the Earl Marshal governors appeared to many to be a further example of such municipal conduct.

As for the particular timing of the headteacher's removal, this coincided with a week in which he, together with a group of governors and Yemeni and Somali refugee students, had spoken at a demonstration on the steps of Sheffield town hall against the impending Asylum Bill. This, which threatened to remove income support, housing benefit and free school meals from those seeking asylum, would impact directly on many children at the school. For example, among those at the demonstration were two Yemeni boys from a family whose house in Aden had been razed to the ground the month before, and who read out a poem about that experience.

Orphan of war
Yesterday my father was killed.
The day before yesterday, my mother.
Today I am an orphan.
I want to cry but I have no tears.
I am only a child.
I am only a child.
Someone please help me.
I want to cry.
I want to cry.
I want to cry.

                              but I have no tears

I want to live
I want to learn

> I want a home.
>
> Where is my love?
>
> Where is my family?
>
> This is my life.
> This is my future.
> I am alone.
> I want to cry[18]

This action, and other fund-raising activities undertaken by the students at the school to raise money to pay for the school meals of those students liable to lose them, were later described by one of the local OFSTED team as 'too political'.

The LEA concedes

Realising its exposed position, the LEA conceded to all four of the governors' demands and apologised for the lack of consultation over the preparation of its commentary for the DfEE on the governors' action plan. It produced the correspondence between itself and the DfEE, while reserving the 'right' not to disclose particular documents on which the DfEE had requested 'confidentiality'—documents which were clearly key to a full understanding of the background and motives for the action. Thus, elements of secrecy remained in what should have been an open and democratic process, and vital information affecting the school was withheld from the governing body responsible for managing it.

Meanwhile, a group of sixteen left Labour parliamentarians, led by the Chesterfield MP, Tony Benn, put down an early day motion in the House of Commons in support of the ex-headteacher and the governors, calling upon 'Sheffield Education Authority to restore to the governors their full powers to act'.[19] This intervention was picked up not only by the mainstream press in Sheffield and the *Yorkshire Post*,[20] but also became the main front-page story on the city-wide free newspaper, the *Sheffield Gazette*,[21] and thus found its way into virtually every home in Sheffield. Blunkett responded by trying to amend the motion in the House, and the chair of the LEA, in tandem with Sheffield Central MP Richard Caborn, wrote an angry letter to the sixteen MPs, criticising them for their 'astonishing attack' and seeking to persuade them to renege on their support for the motion (none did). As Caborn and the LEA chair put it, 'we do not welcome interference from outside the city'—an attitude known only too well by Sheffield's black communities. The letter also stated that the LEA had taken its action against the governors and head 'to avoid the imposition of an Educational Association and the consequent disbanding of the governing body'. Yet nowhere in the correspondence from the DfEE to the LEA that had been withheld from the governors was there any suggestion of such a move. The DfEE had, in fact, written to thank the governors and the head for their 'hard work' in completing the action plan, and to offer them more time after Christmas to amend and improve it. This seemed to make the LEA's assertion that an education association was likely to be imposed not simply economy with the truth, but parsimony itself.

Further pressure was exerted upon the LEA by a city-wide petition in support of the governors and the head, presented to the council in early February, praising, as the *Yorkshire Post* reported,[22] the school's achievement and emphasis upon 'the high moral principles of community, of integration in our multicultural society, of peace among nations and international solidarity'. The petition made the point that, 'one must teach children how to cope in this deeply-riven, I'm-all-right Jack, devil-take-the-hindmost society of ours, but to teach nothing but that is simply to collaborate with the rottenness in our society and ensure its continuance. One must also ... impart an understanding that it is possible for every citizen to do something however little—to bring about a change to a more just, more rational and more humane society by contributing to the community'.[23] The school's fund-raising work for the Kurds, for Bosnia, for the peoples of South Africa, Bangladesh, Kashmir, Pakistan, Guyana and for Iraqi families stranded in Sheffield during the Gulf War was emphasised and seen as a part of a tradition of internationalism in Sheffield.

The impact of the LEA action and the publicity it generated put the survival of the school in even greater peril. The students were clear about the root causes, having lived with the attitudes of some of the staff throughout their time at the school. 'It wasn't reet,' they declared to journalists. Their placards expressed their insights. As the *Sheffield Star* reported of their protest: 'the pupils carried placards saying "teachers helped to fail the school but the head got sacked" and "Shame on the authorities".[24] Their anger was even noted in minutes by OFSTED inspectors when they revisited the school in early February 1996, having been confronted with a group of younger students chanting their opposition to the LEA action.

The aftermath

The announcement of the LEA's concessions signalled an important gain for the governors and was a tribute to their steadfastness. But, despite the public pressure that forced the concessions, the LEA continued to manoeuvre against the existing governors. In doing this, it clearly had the full support of government—a fact later revealed when the Secretary of State for Education, Gillian Shephard, visited Sheffield for the Northern Education Conference at the beginning of 1997. In an interview with the Sheffield *Star*, Mrs. Shephard offered the LEA 'a pat on the back for declaring Earl Marshal a failing school'.[25] The LEA had used its newly grasped power to appoint new governors (including three councillors) to supplement the existing body, undermining its black majority. Subsequently, one of the new white councillor governors was elected as chair, thus denying this school, with 83 per cent of black students, black leadership of its governing body. The new regime at the school (the acting headteacher was one of the local OFSTED inspectors) quickly showed its priorities by stating its intention to 'scrap the school's controversial "no exclusions' policy'.[25] In one incident, local police were called to the school and the arrest—in the classroom—of three Year II Pakistani students was sanctioned, for shouting at the police out of the window. These students were taken to the local Attercliffe police station where they were kept for two hours. One was charged with disorderly behaviour. The *Sheffield Star* reported on its front page that 'one pupil who witnessed the arrests said two of the youths were 'only protesting at the police tactics. One of the lads said, "You can't arrest someone for something like that." And he was arrested too, he claimed.' The report went on to quote an LEA spokesman as saying that 'the new head is determined that such behaviour is not allowed to go on'.[26] As if a harbinger, these Sheffield arrests were followed by a government announcement on the 4, March reported in the *Guardian* on the following day, that 'police powers of stop and arrest would be extended onto school corridors and classrooms. For the first time, officers would be allowed to enter school property without invitation.' *In loco parentis* was superseded by 'sus'.

The issues that the Earl Marshal events threw up were also symptomatic of what was happening at a national level. New Labour and its shadow education secretary were retreating even further from a commitment towards comprehensive education, advocating streaming and 'fast track' approaches for 'gifted' students while blaming the 'old Left'[27] for the failures of inner-city comprehensive schools, and projecting Victorian-style partnerships between well-endowed schools in the private sector and inner-city comprehensives. Such an enterprise would revive the days of nineteenth-century 'settlements', when public schoolboys did their penance and earned their plaudits through charitable days spent in the slums helping the underprivileged.[28] Selection was being actively promoted by shadow health minister Harriet Harman, who, following in the footsteps of Labour leader Tony Blair, sent her son to a grant-maintained school some miles away from where she lived. The principles of inclusive education were further sidelined by the establishment of 'pupil referral units' in major urban areas to be used as segregated resources and dumping grounds for excluded students (disproportionately from black communities). Moreover, such units provide a continuous incitement to exclusion for headteachers, as only permanently excluded students can gain entry. Even OFSTED has had doubts about these:[29] Often they offer only two hours' teaching a day and their curriculum and educational standards are generally extremely low, recalling the days of schools for the 'educationally sub-normal' (ESN) and other such institutions of social and educational rejection.

But more than all these related issues, at the centre of the Earl Marshal dispute was a real parable of how a combination of political interference, backward teacher association interest and LEA embroilment can put an inner-city school into a potentially terminal situation and its community in serious danger of losing its local education resources. For these events carried knowledge and insight about the powers that organise our education resources, both locally and nationally and, as one of the Earl Marshal poets put it in *School of the World*, 'Without the word *know*, the world is a disaster'.[30]

When a supposedly impartial monitoring system such as OFSTED places itself at the centre of such intrigues, teachers and parents need to understand what has happened to the notion of objective assessment of schools and fair inspection free of external constraints and prejudice. It can be no surprise that the tension provoked by an expected visitation from OFSTED habitually dominates schools as more and more of their teachers are menaced by their interventions or subjected in their precious in-service time to routine sessions on 'How to prepare for inspection'—rather than considering the genuine and pressing educational issues that concern the inner-city communities they serve and their students. As for the LEA, which should be the bulwark of support for, and protector of, hard-pressed inner-city schools, its timidity before central government pressure, backward teacher association interest and the New Labour educationalists, can only be seen as a betrayal of the principles on which it is assumed to be founded and the very people it is elected to serve.

As for the students, they continued to demonstrate that they were no longer mere vessels of a passive way of learning and understanding. The success of their first protests in January, and the lingering ethos of a school which had given them confidence and an affirmation of themselves, stayed with them. In April they demonstrated again, boycotting classes on behalf of a Yemeni girl whom, they asserted, had been assaulted and victimised by a racist teacher. As the *Star* of Sheffield reported: 'At the school gates they waved hastily-made banners which claimed racial discrimination by some teachers.'[31] They tasted victory, as the teacher was suspended and never returned to the school. It was further proof that their voices and action were powerful, and could impact effectively upon the system around them,

Then in July, following the appointment of a new headteacher, the students suddenly discovered that the school's logo and watchwords, with which many of them closely identified, had been summarily replaced. The three doves—one black, one white, one brown—rising from an open book, and the line from Bob Marley's *Redemption Song*: 'None but ourselves can free our minds', had gone from the school letters they were given to take home for their parents. In their stead was the old, former logo of Earl Marshal School—the heraldic lion, stolen from Africa by the English aristocracy and used as a royal emblem by the Duke of Norfolk, the 'Earl Marshal' of England and symbolic 'champion' of the monarch. It was a restoration of all that was backward, oppressive and exclusive in the representation of power, and now these students of the world were obliged to wear it as a crest on the newly-imposed school uniform.

But they had an answer as the narrative of their lives, futures and struggle continues. On the last night before the end of what had been a tumultuous school year, using a stencil they had made, they painted the logo of the doves and book across the school entrance—and there, sprayed on the school walls and across the road leading to the main door, were Marley's strong and prophetic words, a message for the present and for the future.

Notes

1 *Guardian* October 1995.
2 *Times Educational Supplement*, 1 July 1994. The targeting of inner London by OFSTED continued into 1996, when a report into primary school literacy in Islington, Tower Hamlets and Southwark was criticised as 'politically slanted' by the LEAs after the chief inspector, Chris Woodhead, had cut some passages and sharpened the report's criticisms. According to Anne Worsley, Southwark's chair of education, the 'pre-planned political agenda' had caused the alteration from a version helpful to schools to one which made political capital. *Guardian*, 7 May 1996.
3 *The Times, 28 October 1995.*
4 Sheffield Education Department, *Report on inspection of Earl Marshal School'*, May 1995, and OFSTED, *Earl Marshal School: a report from the Office of Her Majesty's Chief Inspector of Schools*, July 1995.
5 See the *Guardian*, 5 January 1996, for a report on how the head of OFSTED, Chris Woodhead, had a pamphlet published by 'Politeia, a right-wing think tank', suggesting that LEAs are unnecessary.
6 See article by Kevin Mitchell in the *Observer*, 21 May 1995.
7 See books published by Earl Marshal School, *Valley of Words, 1992, Lives of love and hope, 1993, School of the world, 1994* and *Heart of Sheffield, 1995.*
8 See article by Chris Searle, 'Governors hold the key' in *Adults Learning*, National Organisation for Adult Learning (NIACE), December 1994.
9 De Gruchy's comments were reported in *The Times*, 25 November 1994, and *Guardian*, 23 May 1996 for the Wilding case.
10 *Times Educational Supplement*, 28 April 1995.
11 *Sheffield Telegraph*, 17 February 1995.
12 *Star*, Sheffield, 6 January 1996.
13 *Daily Telegraph, 13 December 1995.*
14 *Asian Times*, 17 February 1996.
15 *Star*, Sheffield, 5 January 1995.
16 *Star*, Sheffield, 9 February 1995 and *Yorkshire Post,* 9 February 1995.
17 From 'Lies' in Yevtushenko, Yevgeni, *Selected Poems*, London, 1962.
18 From unpublished poem by Wiel Mohammed.
19 See House of Commons, *Notice of Motions, 16* January 1996, in the names of Tony Benn, Alan Simpson, Jeremy Corbyn, Diane Abbott, Alice Mahon, Dennis Skinner, Bernie Grant, John Austin-Walker, Max Madden, Chris Mullin, George Galloway, Brian Sedgemore, Peter Hain, Llew Smith, Alan Meale and Robert Wareing.
20 *Yorkshire Post*, 18 January 1996 and *Star*, Sheffield, 18 January 1996.
21 *Sheffield Gazette*, 1 8 January 1996.
22 *Yorkshire Post*, 1 February 1996.

23 Bill Moore, 'In reference to the case of Mr. Chris Searle, late headmaster of Earl Marshal School' (introduction to petition presented to Sheffield city council, 31 January 1996).

24 *Star*, Sheffield, 9 January 1996.

25 *Star*, Sheffield, 2 January 1997.

26 *Star*, Sheffield, 6 January 1996.

27 *Star*, Sheffield, 31 January 1996.

28 *Guardian*, 28 January 1996

29 *Guardian*, 27 December 1995.

30 *Guardian*, 20 December 1995.

31 From 'Know!', a poem by Shahid Khan in *School of the World*, Earl Marshal School, Sheffield, 1994.

32 *Star*, Sheffield, 21 April 1996.

CHRIS SEARLE

During the seventies, Chris Searle's books like *Classrooms of Resistance*, 1976, *The Forsaken Lover*, 1972 or *The World in a Classroom*, 1977, and his approaches to English teaching, creative writing and the pedagogy of anti-racism, were at the centre of the radical movement in British education.

Until recently the headteacher of an inner city comprehensive school in Sheffield, he was involved on a daily basis in directly withstanding and struggling against the deeply damaging effects of Conservative legislation falling upon inner city schools and the communities they serve.

Chris Searle was born in Romford, England in 1944, and has taught in East London, Sheffield, Canada, Mozambique and Grenada. He is now a Lecturer of English in Education at Goldsmiths' College, University of London.

Among his books are *The Forsaken Lover: White Worlds and Black People*, winner of the Martin Luther King Award, 1972, *Classrooms of Resistance, The World in a Classroom, 'We're Building the New School!: Diary of a Teacher in Mozambique, Words Unchained: Language and Revolution in Grenada, Grenada Morning* and *A Blindfold Removed: Ethiopia's Struggle for Literacy.*

He is a member of the editorial advisory committee and frequent contributor to the international journal, *Race and Class*.